CONNECTED

The 12 Ways of Wellbeing for a
Holistically Healthy Life

Gemma Margerison

A CIP catalogue record for this book is available from the British Library.

Front cover design by Ariane Sherine.

Published by Juliette Jones Editorial Services
Juliette.Jones@outlook.com
www.juliettejones.co.uk

Contents

For Harper, Ronnie, Edie, and Mia;
may you always believe that anything is possible.

CHAPTER ONE

Introduction

Everything is connected. If the Covid-19 pandemic of 2020 taught us anything, it is that, as human beings, we do not naturally function or survive in isolation. We have learnt all too well the harsh reality of the effects of separation on physical, mental, and emotional health; on our relationships and friendships; on our jobs, finances, and activities; and, for some, on the ability to see the possibility of the future. We need connection. Connection to our bodies and minds to keep us healthy and well; connection to our immediate and wider communities for companionship and camaraderie; connection to nature for energy and sustenance; and connection to a sense of tenacity and perseverance to give us hope.

Self, others, world, and purpose. These are the four spheres with which we need to have a connection in order to achieve a rounded and holistic sense of wellbeing. Within each of these areas lies a multitude of interwoven facets, the combination of which is as unique to everyone as their own fingerprint, but all four spheres must be present. For many of my clients, this way of thinking is a revelation. Traditionally, there has been a lot of emphasis on wellbeing as diet and exercise, but now we are coming to understand that, while these are crucial elements to the foundations of a healthy life, they neglect to incorporate both the areas that are blatantly as impactful, as well as some of the more subtle and softer sets of skills.

Wellbeing is one of the results of the ongoing process of taking care of your body, mind, and soul; of understanding yourself, the good, the bad, and the downright weird; of accepting yourself just as you are by believing that you have worth and value; and of empowering yourself to be able to make choices and decisions based upon your particular set of needs. This process begins with knowledge, and that is the purpose of this book, a passing on of knowledge not just from my own learning and experiences, but from the expertise of the businesses, organisations, and charities who have kindly contributed their valuable inputs.

From relationship coaches and equine therapists to mortgage advisors and youth workers, from writers and artists to advocates, assistants to ambassadors, the wealth of information, advice, and guidance that has been donated to this book continues to blow me away, as does the passion each contributor has shown for this project and for advancing the message of wellbeing; I cannot thank each and every one of them enough. Each contributor has been able to publish their websites and social media handles. Please take the time to like, follow, and share their work, they absolutely deserve it.

Thank you also to those who have stood by me as I have pulled this project together, who have supported me in so many ways, and who have believed in and encouraged me; I would not be here without you. Particular thanks go to my partner, Scott, and our immediate families for all they have put up with. Finally, I want to thank everyone who has purchased, been given, or borrowed this book. I hope you get the same joy from reading it as I from writing it; it has taught me so much.

Gemma Margerison
Author, speaker, coach, and researcher

CHAPTER TWO

The Four Spheres of Connection

In 2015, I was diagnosed with mild Post-Traumatic Stress Disorder (PTSD). The how and the why are not important or relevant here, except to say that this is where my love affair with wellbeing truly began. It was there in the depths of my darkest hour that the thought of helping others sparked a light in me that, for a brief moment, I had believed would never return. It gave me a sense of purpose, a way to give back, and I am grateful for the fact this notion has been my guiding star from that moment on.

Since then, my journey to my current role, as with my journey to recovery, has been a bumpy one. However, I am pleased to say that I no longer suffer from the symptoms that led me to the GP surgery that warm July, and I now run three thriving businesses that bring me joy, sadness, frustration, and pride on a day-to-day basis; and on top of that, have allowed me to support individuals from all backgrounds and walks of life to also find their joy again.

I am first and foremost a coach, specifically The Resilience and Recovery Coach for Gemma Louise Coaching, which I began in 2019. From the feedback I received and the passion I felt for coaching, I took the business full-time from January 2020 after leaving a role within an engineering company. If my time in the corporate world taught me anything, it is that I loved the one-to-one interactions I had with people who needed to talk. This led me to begin a Doctorate in Coaching and Mentoring at Oxford Brookes University, through which I reached Post-Graduate Diploma level.

Since going self-employed, I have supported numerous clients who have been through trauma and difficulty from historic abuse to toxic relationships, from marriage breakdowns to surviving critical illness and injury. I have seen some incredible outcomes, for which I cannot take any credit. The sheer determination and growth required to leave unhealthy relationships or start new healthy ones, to go back to university or to gain new employment, to move to the other side of the country or to simply believe in and love yourself, is not something I can control; I can only be a sounding board and provide tools when required.

Gemma Louise Coaching has become a success because of the people I have worked with; there is not a session that goes by that I do not learn something about myself or something I can do to improve the services I offer. I am proud to have been able to walk alongside these individuals for as long as they have needed me, and then be able to see them reach a level of independence and go it alone. The purpose of Gemma Louise Coaching is to improve strength, confidence, and wellness in those who have experienced trauma and difficulty so that they might reach their full potential; I know they will all do incredibly well.

My second business is Trauma Resilience and Recovery for Uniformed, Care, and Emergency Services, which can thankfully be shortened to TRUCE. I began working with armed forces veterans in late 2013 and have done so on and off ever since. This community was not only fantastically supportive of me as I went through my PTSD struggles, but it continues to be a source of inspiration, motivation, and instruction. I have been additionally fortunate in that I have also worked with serving personnel and military spouses, particularly in early 2021, which prompted my expansion into other frontline staff.

TRUCE provides resilience training, trauma debriefing, and follow up coaching for anyone who lives in service of others, and I have had the privilege of working with the NHS, police, local authority adult services, care homes, and youth workers in addition to the military. The My Resilient Service Masterclass training package I offer has added value to the work that is already being done to support staff within these organisations, and an outsider perspective has proven to provide a new and different way of looking at things.

While TRUCE is not yet as established as Gemma Louise Coaching, it has enormous potential. My hope is to specialise my further studies to prove its benefits within the populations it seeks to serve, and to expand its reach further still, particularly towards Fire and Rescue, and the farming communities. The Covid-19 pandemic has taught us the importance of our frontline, care, and uniformed services, and I believe that now is the time for positive change, for more support, and for the recognition of the sacrifices being made to keep the rest of the population safe and well.

Finally, I am a writer and a speaker. I have always loved writing and was first published in a collection of poetry gathered from local primary schools in the area I grew up in. Reading, writing, and stories got me through those awkward teenage years of too many emotions, and I went on to complete an undergraduate degree in Creative Writing and English Literature taking inspiration for my dissertation from the trip to Uganda I took in the summer of my second year. Being a published author was always the dream.

However, my writing career took me into journalism, working for a small national newspaper in Auckland, New Zealand. My love of story led me to interview politicians, sports stars, music legends and upcoming artists, charity workers, thought leaders, and professionals of all kinds. However, it became clear that I lacked a certain bloodhound instinct for a juicy story, and, while I do not regret my time in the profession, I decided not to continue in the field once I returned back to the UK. Instead, I put those skills into creating newsletters for programmes I worked in across multiple businesses.

The more involved I became in working with wellbeing, the further away I drifted from the fiction that I used to adore, and began to channel some self-help into my writing. Just before the first lockdown in 2020, I was published in a collaborative book called Unzenable: A Guide to Stress Less & Be More and during the rest of the year I was featured in some magazines talking about mental health and wellness. Now, we have the publication of Connected which is a dream come true and I hope it is not the last book to have my name on the front cover.

I have also travelled across the country for guest speaking engagements talking about my personal recovery journey, my work in wellbeing, and also my unique model of resilience. It is not always easy to communicate the more vulnerable aspects of my story, however, my motto has always been this: if it helps prevent even just one person from getting to the stage I got to, then it is worth it. Sharing real life experience is where the connection happens, and it usually only takes someone to be brave to spark much needed conversation in this area.

While these hats all seem very different, there are three distinct and important threads weaving them all together: trauma, resilience, and wellbeing. This book focuses on the last of those three things, and I think that is a very timely place to start. Wellbeing was brought to the forefront of our minds during the Covid-19 pandemic; many of us became aware, perhaps for the first time, that wellbeing was not simply an optional extra or a nice-to-have perk in the workplace. Instead, we learnt that wellbeing is essential to living healthy lives.

As I mentioned in Chapter 1, when I ask about wellbeing or I hear discussions on how to promote it, the go-to answers are often around diet and exercise, with some mention of mental health. Through years of research and reading, I began to understand that wellbeing consisted of so much more than what we had originally thought, and that there are numerous aspects of life that influence, impact, and improve our wellbeing if we connect with them in the right way. And so, I began to explore what the key areas were, ending up with what I call 'The Four Spheres of Connection: self, others, world, and purpose'.

As these developed, I knew I had to drill down to what was involved in each of the four and came across a tool used to measure wellness in different areas of life. This tool comes in many different forms and goes by many different names, and while it was great resource to me when I first started coaching, I quickly began to understand that its six to eight sections on average, did not fully explain what I had seen to be true through The Four Spheres of Connection. Therefore, I set about adding to this until I had something that I believed fully represented wellbeing as a whole: The Wellbeing Wheel.

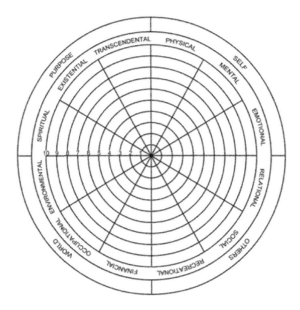

With 12 areas of wellbeing now at my fingertips, dividing neatly into the four spheres, I finally had something that I could use to help people look at wellbeing in a different way; not a tool that asked us to judge or rate every area of our lives, but one that gave us a complete understanding of holistic wellbeing and allowed us to monitor our levels of connection, and how healthy those levels were. It is important to note here that perfection is never what we are asking or looking for with The Wellbeing Wheel, it is simply a tool for discussion.

When I started teaching The Wellbeing Wheel, I also had to be able to comprehensively define what each of the twelve areas meant and what was included in them from the perspective of wellbeing. Starting with the first sphere, Physical Wellbeing looks at your relationship with your diet, exercise, and sleep as well as the regularity with which you engage with health and medical check-ups such as dentist visits. It also considers how you value yourself and how you view yourself physically as that often has an impact on how healthy this particular part of your wellbeing is.

Mental Wellbeing centres not just around the health of your thoughts but also on you seeking opportunities to learn, mentally challenging yourself, and being able to apply techniques in order to stay stable during difficulty. Mental health concerns or conditions are taken into account here, but there are so many things we can do to engage our brains in daily life if we only look for them. These are good for long-term brain function as well as the development of skills, knowledge, and experience.

Emotional Wellbeing has a couple of elements to it. The first is around the ability to regulate the way that you feel, and to choose emotional responses that are appropriate and proportionate to the situation rather than seeing red and flying off the handle. The second is about being able to spot emotional changes in others, and having the confidence and compassion to reach out and ask if they are ok. The third is knowing how, when, and where to seek support for yourself, or for others, if you need it.

Moving on to the second sphere, we have Relational Wellbeing. This element asks you to consider your romantic or sexual relationships and whether they are safe, and if there is mutual respect and honesty. For single individuals, it is about your ability to be comfortable in your own company, being able to pursue relations in the right way for the right reasons, and being able to recognise potential red flags. Immediate family are also included in this section, and again, this is about trust and making time for each other.

Social Wellbeing is about your wider interactions with friends, extended family, work colleagues or business associates, and the wider community in general. Again, this looks at mutual respect plus kindness, care, and the intentional setting aside of time for each other. Social anxiety or fears related to close proximity with others as a result of the Covid-19 pandemic can make social wellness more difficult, however, we are more connected online than ever, and solutions can be found to ensure that nobody is alone.

Recreational Wellbeing looks at sports, hobbies, and interests; anything that you do to relax, unwind, or get your heart pumping. It requires the undertaking of safe and healthy activities, balanced with the challenge of trying something new, and having things that you would like to try or get involved in. Many new experiences involve new people, new skills, and new ways to unwind. Therefore, it is easy to see here the links between this section and some of the others we have looked at so far, which makes it a great time to point out that many of these sections interweave, cross over, and influence each other.

In the third sphere, we have Financial Wellbeing, which is not about having a lot of money. Instead, financial wellbeing considers the stability of income, your potential to have savings, and your knowledge of key financial considerations such as loans, mortgages, and investments. Being financially well is also about having someone you can talk to about money and not letting things like debt cause you ill mental health. Being able to make sound, well informed, and planned financial decisions can save a lot of grief.

Occupational Wellbeing is again about stability paired with the challenge and growth of being able to learn something new and move up the ladder if that is something you desire. A healthy workplace should help its employees feel valued, and in turn, employees should get a sense of satisfaction from the tasks they undertake. For some, work is the means to an end rather than a calling, which is perfectly fine too; the most important part is that it gives you what you need and keeps you safe and healthy.

Environmental Wellbeing is another section that has multiple layers to it. The first is your connection with your immediate environment and whether it is safe, clean, and allows you access to the things you need. The second is your interaction with the local environment and making environmentally conscious decisions when shopping or being out in nature. The third is the global environment which considers causes or charities out in the world that you connect with and the things you do to support their work.

In the final sphere, we have Spiritual Wellbeing. Whilst this is less about religion and more about presence, grounding, and reflection, the notion of spirituality is not completely discounted from the mix. It is about the things that bring you calm and peace, and how often you prioritise those activities. I think you might be surprised with the contributions I have placed in this chapter, but these have been put there intentionally and I hope the link will make sense to you as you reach that point in the book. Being present is a present.

Existential Wellbeing is literally as simple as knowing your reason for being and understanding what gets you out of bed in the morning. Also, this takes into account what you do to contribute to something that leaves a legacy, and being able to find enough hope to continue regardless of what life might throw at you. Now this does not have to go as far as being able to answer the great questions around the meaning of life, but rather creating meaning in life, whatever that might look like for you: children, art, business, etc.

Last but not least, is Transcendental Wellbeing which looks at the things that give you the feeling of being taken away to another place. It is about understanding what inspires you, what motivates you, and what gives you that feeling of awe and wonder. For some, this might be climbing to the top of a mountain to look at the view; for others, it is curling up with a good book. Similar to Spiritual Wellbeing, there is also a consideration around how much opportunity you allow yourself to do the things that make you feel that way.

However, I did not just want to have an academic model, a chart on a piece of paper; I wanted to bring it to life. And so, the idea for Connected was born; with the notion that while I had created the model, I was not an expert in all these fields, but I bet I knew people that were. Over the next twelve months I met, connected with, spoke to, and signed up the 45 contributors that have made this book what it is today; somewhere between a self-help book and a curated wellbeing directory of knowledgeable individuals who can help you develop the areas that speak to you.

You can use this book in two ways: either reading it from start to finish which is a sure-fire way of learning something new and being able to soak up all that this book has to offer, or you can find the chapter, or chapters, that you think will be relevant for you in your personal situation and start there. This book is designed to be an entry-level welcome into the world of wellbeing and so I have tried to keep it as accessible, reader-friendly, and jargon-free as I possibly could. However, I would love to hear from you if you have any questions.

My final point on introducing you to The Four Spheres of Connection is that they are not, nor are they intended to be, a recipe for happiness. Happiness is an emotion, and therefore it comes and goes depending on our individual circumstances or the situation in which we find ourselves. The notion that we could or should be happy all the time is, to me, nonsense, and the pursuit of happiness as a constant state of being only causes us to be worn out and disappointed. Instead, the purpose of this model is to start you on the journey to wellness.

I am very excited that we are going to go on this journey together, starting with Part 1: Connection to Self. While the bulk of the chapters are packed with the information, advice, and guidance from our contributors, I will be adding my reflections and learning points at the end of each one. Are you sitting comfortably? Ok, let's go!

PART ONE

Connection to the Self

CHAPTER THREE

Physical Wellbeing

"Health is wealth, and success needs a healthy mind and body to be sustained and enjoyed," says Julia Riewald, Owner of Julia Riewald, a success and health coaching business. "I am helping busy individuals and corporate organisations, who understand and value health as a key factor to success, to elevate their total wellbeing, physical fitness and agility, and mental acuity." As the daughter of a GP, Julia says she took a total fascination to the human body from a young age. "I am passionate about research and learning how nutrition feeds our bodily engine to help us enjoy life to our full potential," she says.

In her early career, Julia found that whatever job or position she held within her corporate business, she always seemed to find herself in a coaching or development position. "Becoming a Success and Health Coach is the result of combining my passion for the body and food with the love for empowering others," she says. "I believe that we can all live a better life and be more productive at home and at work if we have less health issues and worries, so I share my knowledge to empower others to make the best choices for themselves and become the best version of themselves."

"Gut health issues, cancers, diabetes, and heart attacks are only a few of the conditions that my ancestors, family, myself, and even my horse, can suffer from. And not only suffer but hugely reduce quality of life, and even lead to death," says Julia. "Help your body and it will do miracles for you." Gut health and nutrigenetics are two areas especially close to Julia's heart, and seeing the great results in her clients on a day-to-day basis, their improved quality of life, fuels her desire to share these hints and tips with as many people as possible.

"With a business corporate background, I understand the importance and need for top mental acuity to make the right decisions and cope with the pressures corporate life can bring. Keeping staff healthier, more focused, and improving their energy will deliver better results, lead to more efficient workflow, and create more motivated teams, and thus, help improve the organisations overall productivity," says Julia. "We are all diligent regarding the maintenance of the assets and tools we need for our day-to-day, we follow the user manual and maintain and service everything to get long use from it. A successful life and business must see the body and must consider health as the most important asset."

To help her clients Julia uses a Lifestyle Analysis to choose the optimum fit for the individual from a choice of fully supported, transformational programmes combining science, nutrition, and mindfulness so they benefit from performing at their personal best and improving their mental and physical potential. "Gut microbiome health, DNA nutrigenetics, and cardiovascular support form core elements of the programmes," she says. "They help to achieve health benefits like better sleep, more energy, elevated mental acuity and focus, improved weight management, reduced aches and pains, reduced menopause symptoms, and less struggles with autoimmune diseases or Inflammatory Bowel Disease (IBD) issues."

Julia can offer a thirty-minute, free, no obligation, initial consultation and Lifestyle Analysis to explore the best way forward for clients and maximise the benefits for them. Julia also provides a holistic online health journey through Percent-Edge.com. Percent-Edge combines science, nutrition, and mindfulness with programmes built around individual's lifestyle in order to improve their health and performance. "These are delivered with a concierge level of service to help you become the best version of yourself," she says. "Every user receives, in addition to one-to-one mentoring, a bespoke programme delivered through a personal online portal to support their journey to better health and wellbeing."

Finally, Julia coaches therapists, other coaches, and personal trainers to utilise these programmes and add extra value to their clients' journey of health. "The programmes are complimentary to existing services and product portfolios, and are providing a method to achieve anticipated results significantly faster and better. This helps the clients and increases the therapist's or coach's reputation, making it a win-win for therapists, or coaches, and their clients," she says.

Julia believes that good health and wellbeing is a result of our daily lifestyle choices, a balance of mind, body, and spirit; three elements that work closely together. Julia's focus is the body and nutrition, and, specifically, these three areas: gut microbiome, DNA nutrigenetics, and cardiovascular health. "An out-of-balance microbiome is said to be the root cause of all disease. I get asked what is a microbiome and why is DNA so important? Well, a microbiome is an acquired ecosystem of bacteria, fungi, and microorganisms that live in us and on us. It forms about 90% of who we are, i.e., we are only about 10% human," she says.

Two-thirds of the microbiome is said to live in your gut, so it is easy to understand that if two-thirds, so almost all, of you is out of balance, it will have an impact on your overall health and wellbeing. "Scientists have discovered that the microbiome is linked to almost every bodily system," says Julia. "It affects your: immunity, as 70% of your immune cells are birthed in the gut and trained by the good bacteria as to what to react to and what to accept in the body; digestion and metabolism, as the bacteria help to absorb nutrients; mental health, as the microbiome influences how we think, feel, what we do and desire; and, genetic expression, as in the behaviour of our genes related to utilising nutrients."

DNA on the other hand is a long thread-like molecule which acts as our body's own instruction manual. And whilst we have long known that it defines things like the colour of your eyes, the size of your feet and more; new discoveries are looking at the areas in the DNA that are essential for your health and that define what your body can or cannot do with the nutrients you eat. Nutrigenetics is studying this part of the DNA and simple saliva tests now allow to determine what foods, nutrients, and supplements are beneficial to you and which are not so good. This enables us to make the best food and lifestyle choices for our individual bodies based on science and fact. No more guess work. But why is balancing your microbiome and knowing your DNA so important?

"Let's imagine a car," says Julia. "We regularly service the fuelling system such as the filters, tank, and pipework to have a safe, successful ride and prevent breaking down. Our gut is for the body what the fuelling system is for the car, only much more sophisticated and in need of daily 'servicing'. It is here where food/body fuel is filtered, metabolised and unwanted elements passed out the other end so that our bodily engine gets all the nutrients it needs, is not overloaded with toxins, and can work most efficiently. So, if the gut is not enabled to work well and our microbiome is out of balance, which is called dysbiosis, we are not getting all of the nutrients from the food or even the medication that we need."

All sorts of issues can occur from dysbiosis. "Leaky gut is when our gut walls are compromised and damaged to the extent that toxins and undigested food particles 'leak' into our bloodstream. These particles will cause mild herds of inflammation anywhere they settle, and it is this constant underlying inflammation that causes bigger problems and leads to feeling unwell, bad sleep, low mood and energy, brain-fog, weight issues, irritable bowel syndrome (IBS), bloating, diabetes, heart disease, arthritis, autoimmune diseases, and allergies to name but a few of the symptoms that would trouble our everyday life experience," says Julia. Mood, immune response, and genes are also affected in other ways linked to the gut.

"The gut is closely connected to the brain via a 'communication highway' called the Vagus Nerve. In fact," says Julia, "there is much more messaging going from the gut to the brain than the other way around." Bacteria in the gut, as we have explored, helps with breaking down and metabolising your food, and sends messages to your brain which can determine your mood, from happy to depressed; your behaviour, from shy to bold; and even dictate what you want to eat. Cravings, therefore, are not what you think you need to eat, but rather the bacteria begging for food.

Julia teaches that gut health is also significantly impacting your immune response; your hormonal balance, with over 70% of hormones being produced and metabolised in the gut; and your genes, i.e., how your genes behave. "Nutrigenetics helps us to determine the right 'fuel' for each individual. Just as you would not fill diesel into a petrol engine, an apple a day might be a healthy choice for one person but not for another. Why? We all have over 2000 little genetic 'defects' or spelling mistakes in our instruction manual, and these can mean that we cannot activate or metabolise certain vitamins so the body can actually make use of it," she says.

B vitamins, Coenzyme Q10, caffeine, vitamin D, Omega 3, iron and lactose are all well-known elements of our nutrition, but they can only support our health if the body has the right script in its DNA to allow the genes to effectively use them. "For example, you might show good enough levels of B12 in your blood, but if you cannot metabolise it, your body will not get it and you will develop a deficiency. Coffee, if you are able to genetically benefit from it, then the antioxidant properties can delay the onset of breast cancer in women by up to seven years. Omega 3, albeit very important for your blood flow, your brain and more, can lead to an increase in cholesterol levels in about 13% of individuals who have a faulty APOA1 gene," says Julia.

"Testing and knowing, not guessing, is a new power that we have to elevate health and prevent illness and nutrient deficiencies. Knowing your genetic code allows you to focus on foods and lifestyle choices, and stops you from wasting time and money on nutrients and supplements your body simply cannot utilise," says Julia. Therefore, her top tip is to listen to your body and 'service' it better than any other asset you are using. "Our body is sending us messages, and we need to listen out for the 'rattling noises' just as you would hear strange noises in your car when something is not ok," she says.

Yet, while we would take our car immediately to the garage to find the sources of issues and fix them, when we feel tired, experience bad sleep, pile on weight for no obvious reason, struggle with brain fog or lack of energy, or even develop pain and illness, we look for an explanation like a stressful job or kids, doing too much exercise, going through menopause, or we put it down to age. We often accept the pain and continue on. Julia urges us to wake up and pay attention. These are the rattling noises your body is sending you to say "Hey, I am a bit off balance here. Please have a look at me so I can work properly again". A Lifestyle Analysis is one way to do this, and in most cases, it is a fantastic start to the journey of better health.

"The genes load the gun, but the lifestyle pulls the trigger," says Julia. "So, if you are serious about a life full of vitality, agility, and mental acuity, then prevention is better than cure. Have a DNA nutrigenetics test done, and find out what genetic type you are and how you can balance genetic 'imperfections' through the right food and exercise choices. However, do some research into the company you are choosing for the test. Most companies have not got their own labs and might sell your data on for research, and cannot really help you explain the impact of your genetic code; they might just leave you with a paper full of numbers and letters for you to figure out what it means."

Julia also offers the following five general health and wellbeing tips. Firstly, destress and be more mindful. "Stress shuts down your bodily business; it effects your immune response, your digestive system, and nervous system to name just the big areas. Take 2-5 minutes and be mindful of the moment. Do this multiple times a day. Start small and build up. There are great focussing exercises for the eyes, breathing exercises like box breathing or 3-4-5 breathing. Relax, do what works for you whether that's yoga, listening to music, reading a book, going for a run, or petting a dog; me-time is so important to help our gut get back in balance," she says.

Secondly, exercise. Thirty minutes a day and ideally outside helps to keep your gut moving and exposes you to more bacterial variety which is important for good immune responses. Whenever possible, take the stairs or park the car away from the supermarket entrance, every little helps.

The third tip is to drink plenty of fluid. "We tend to not drink enough or not enough of the right things. Reduce fizzy drinks and juices, and have alcohol in moderation. Water is important. Add fresh fruit pieces like apple slices, berries, and melon or herbs like mint or ginger, or even squeeze a fresh lemon into the water to make a tasty drink," says Julia.

Next, read the label. "Marketing can sell us rat poison and make us believe it is good for our health. Making healthier food choices begins with the awareness of what we are actually eating," says Julia. "'Sugar-free' usually means the use of artificial sweeteners. 'Fat-free' can mean a higher Glycaemic Index than semi-skimmed or full fat. 'Added vitamins' often means that artificial vitamins are added and often there aren't enough to make a difference anyway. Try to replace ready meals with fresh produce, and buy produce that is in season or opt for frozen as they often contain more nutrients. Try to eat organic to reduce the toxic load on the body, but be aware that organic does not mean more nutrients."

And finally, go back to basics in the household. Julia believes we need to cut back on cleaners, personal hygiene products and air-fresheners. "Our generation is obsessed with scents and things that kill 99% of bacteria. Often soap and water will do the job nicely and with no toxic effect on your body, especially your skin, respiratory system, endocrine system, etc. Artificially scented candles, room sprays and alike are a 24/7 exposure to toxins for your body. Opening the doors and windows for 10 minutes twice a day to let fresh air circulate through the rooms is a much healthier and cheaper way, and it actually smells nice too," she says.

"Whatever you do," says Julia. "Always remember, baby steps. Just do it, start somewhere or somehow, you do not need to be an expert overnight. Every little step will take you in the new direction. Also, do what suits you, what feels right for you. This is your life, and you are the only person who really knows how everything feels. Try new things but listen to your body." Remember you can find all of Julia's details as well as some of her top tips in the end of chapter summary.

Listening to your body not only increases your chances of success but also reduces risk of injury. This is something that Rebecca Woolley-Wildgoose, Owner of North Lakes Sports Therapy wishes people would pay more attention to. "The advice I always give to people looking to improve their health and wellbeing is to listen to their body and react accordingly. If you need to rest or your body is in pain, allow that to dictate how you organise your day, week, or month. Rest is so important to the way your body repairs itself so if that means not going for that 5-mile run for a day then listen to your body and give it time to rest," she says.

North Lakes Sports Therapy focuses on two distinct aspects of health and wellbeing: the prevention of injury and the rehabilitation back to optimum levels of functional and sport specific fitness, regardless of age and ability. "My journey towards a health and wellbeing lifestyle and passion started from a personal place," says Rebecca. "I have always loved being outdoors and took up fell running when we moved to the Lake District. I always knew the importance of remaining healthy and in good physical condition for my sport. However, it was my love of helping people become pain free and achieve things they never thought they would be able to that really solidified my career choice."

Rebecca is now a fully qualified Level 5 Sports Therapist. "The aim of sports therapy is to work mainly using musculoskeletal techniques, combined with sport specific massage to manipulate soft tissue. This is connective tissue that has not hardened into bone and cartilage; it includes skin, muscles, tendons, ligaments and fascia. Sports therapy is designed to assist in correcting problems and imbalances in soft tissues that are caused from repetitive and strenuous physical activity, and/or trauma following surgery or injury. The application of sports therapy techniques helps enhance performance, aid recovery, and prevent injury," she says.

Utilising these principles of sport and exercise science, and incorporating physiological and pathological processes, North Lakes Sports Therapy works to help either rehabilitate or prepare individuals for training, competition and everyday life. "We aim to promote physical wellbeing by working with an individual to achieve a specific fitness goal to get back to optimum fitness. Whether you want to be pain free or to run a marathon, I can help you achieve that goal," says Rebecca.

"The main joy in my job is working closely with people, getting to know them, and being able to give them treatment and advice that, for some, makes a big difference in the way they lead their life. I see clients who have been living with chronic pain due to a postural imbalance, a runner who has gone over on their ankle one too many times, or a cyclist who has compromised flexibility in their lower back from being bent over the tri bars. I ensure that each individual I see is equipped with clear expectations of their progress and a plan of how to get them where they want to be."

With that in mind Rebecca has these final pieces of advice. "Eating well, getting plenty of fresh air, and looking after your mental health are such vital parts of personal wellbeing. Another, which is vital to the work that I do as a sports therapist, is to do the exercises your therapist gives you; the more you do them, the better your improvement will be," she says. This combination of good food and exercise is a common theme across the chapter so far and is echoed again by our next contributor.

Adam Grayston is a Body and Mindset Coach working online with busy women around the world on diet and weight loss. "My 12-week programme is centred around helping busy women lose up to 20 pounds in 12 weeks," he says. "This is without dieting, and without needing to go to the gym, if you choose not to go. I also help them build the habits they need to maintain the results long term." Adam's clients receive one-to-one coaching to promote a healthier mindset, assess and discuss lifestyle choices, explore how they feel about themselves, and set small, achievable goals.

"A lifelong passion of using exercise and simple healthy eating to help people feel confident and enjoy life to the fullest was the driving force behind me entering the health and fitness industry almost ten years ago," says Adam. "I worked as a gym instructor, cleaning floors, mopping up sweat and cleaning down machines. Then, I went on to being a personal trainer. After that, I invested a lot of money into becoming a speaker, and a transformation coach."

When he started his career, Adam quickly realised that many women were struggling to keep the weight off and eat good food consistently. "Statistics suggest that at any one time 50% of women are on a diet, and the women that do diet programmes generally do around three a year. On top of that, 1 in 3 teenage girls have apparently either tried to diet or considered going on a diet. So that just shows you how much diets, or juicing, or detoxes, or weight loss are part and parcel of society, and a lot of it is aimed at women," he says.

A woman's body works slightly differently to a man's body. Women typically gain weight quicker and tend to carry extra weight because of hormones and reproductive reasons. "There are a lot of women who have grown up with dieting. They have seen parents dieting, or family members, or other women, seen it in magazines, on TV, everywhere. There's billions and billions of pounds being spent promoting diet," says Adam. However, it is not all good.

"There's a lot of information out there about weight loss and the vast majority of it, you just don't need to know. You sign up for weight loss programmes, weight loss groups, juicing programmes, detoxes, and get all these pieces of information, but none of it is specific to you, or none of it is trying to show you what you actually need to put in your body, or how much of it, and how to make it sustainable," he says. According to Adam good eating habits and a good diet starts with food you actually enjoy.

"There's no point in eating things you don't enjoy just for the sake of being healthy. That is one of the fastest ways that you can demotivate yourself."

Adam also has three top tips to help us engage better with our eating habits. "The one at the top of the list is knowing exactly how much you need to put into the body. Get to know what your own calorie intake should be. Because when you find out what your calorie intake is, you have got something to work towards," he says. The next is protein. "A lot of people tend to be protein deficient; they don't have enough protein in their eating habits on a day-to-day basis," says Adam.

"It's really, really important because your body is made up of a huge amount of muscle and that's something that it wants to keep up. Protein helps your muscles and helps your body to feel satisfied and feel full, because it's been fed properly." Almost everything in your body needs protein, so this is a key part of Adam's message. "Protein really curbs your cravings for sugar and junk food. So, the second thing is getting that protein, and again, if you use the calculator online, it will tell you exactly what you should be aiming for each day in terms of protein. It makes a massive, massive, massive, massive difference," he says.

The third tip is exercise. "You want to be exercising and burning calories, but you don't have to do a difficult or a long workout. If you can only fit in 10 or 15 minutes a day, that is where you start from. Over time you can slowly build up from that," says Adam. "You don't have to do a lot of exercise to lose weight and get great results; start really, really small and then build up from that. Try and find some beginner workouts to do online or follow a beginner's class. Something like 20 minutes, something simple and straightforward for the newbies. You can find it, you can find workouts like that everywhere online."

Chapter summary

Like a lot of people, I have parts of my body that I am not a big fan of; I have emotional snacking habits that require continuous management, and I have days where the thought of getting out and doing some exercise makes me feel ill. However, my relationship and connection with physical health changed for the better with the discovery of a single phrase, "eat like you love yourself", and for me this taught me three things:

Firstly, not to punish my body for whatever else is going on in my life just because it is something I can control. As has been highlighted in this chapter, what you put in determines what you get out so filling my body full of nasties is not going to make anything better. Natural, clean, mindful eating tailored to my individual needs is the way forward, and each day I take a step closer to achieving this. Less sugar, more protein has been particularly helpful for my journey.

Secondly, to be more aware of pain or discomfort and not to see it as something to be afraid of. Pain does not always have to mean there is something to panic about, nor should pain be ignored or treated as a weakness. I know we have heard this before, but pain is a message that needs to be translated so find someone who can help if you need it. Whether it is a doctor, dentist, healer, or therapist, there are so many avenues available for you to find the right treatment and support.

Thirdly and finally, to be kind to yourself mentally and emotionally. No, I have not put this in the wrong chapter. A little kindness goes a long way with physical wellbeing, especially if we have goals to work towards. Missing leg day or exceeding your daily calorie count is not the end of the world, you can try again tomorrow. Similarly, you do not have to stick with something that is not working. Listen to your body, understand with kindness, and respond with what is right for you. This, I believe, is physical wellness.

In this chapter you have heard from...

Name: Julia Riewald
Name of company: Julia Riewald
Position in company / Job title: Owner
Company website: https://www.percent-edge.com/jr
Facebook: @julia.riewald or @ThroughLifestyle
Instagram: @julia_riewald
LinkedIn: https://www.linkedin.com/in/julia-riewald/

Name: Rebecca Woolley-Wildgoose
Name of company: North Lakes Sports Therapy
Position in company / Job title: Owner / Therapist

Company website: www.northlakessportstherapy.co.uk
Facebook: @northlakesmobiletherapy
Instagram: @northlakesmobiletherapy

Name: Adam Grayston
Name of company: Adam Grayston Body and Mindset Coach
Position in company / Job title: Owner
Company website: adamgrayston.co.uk
Facebook: @adamgraystontransformations
Instagram: @thedietdestroyer
LinkedIn: https://www.linkedin.com/in/adamgrayston/

CHAPTER FOUR

Mental Wellbeing

Kelly Farr joined the Royal Air Force in 2003 when she was just shy of 25 years old; she served for 17 years as an Avionics Engineer. "My final posting was at RAF Cosford, from January 2015 to March 2020. This base was the RAF Home of Engineering and I spent the initial three and a half years of this posting training new aircraft technicians," she says. "During this time, I completed a Neuro-Linguistic Programming (NLP) Practitioner course and, oh wow, it completely changed my life; I understood so much more about other people and, more importantly, about myself!"

Kelly says that something inside her had sparked during the six days of NLP training and subconsciously she knew that her life would take a very different path from then on. "Alongside my role as an Avionics Instructor, a few months post my NLP Practitioner course, I started delivering a five-day Human Performance Course at RAF Cosford, on behalf of another Squadron on base. I did this alongside Jamie, who now happens to be my husband and my business partner! This course had the most incredible, life-changing impact on the participants; their words not mine."

As one of two sets of instructors for the course, the pair trained hundreds of students from across the Ministry of Defence (MOD) and Tri-Service arena. "We absolutely loved the content we were delivering and decided that when we both eventually left the military, we would launch our own training company. We did not know what we would deliver at this stage, it was a fledgling idea. Over the course of the next year, which happened to be my final year serving in the RAF, something amazing happened. The Squadron I delivered the Human Performance training for, asked me if I would like to go and work there full-time," says Kelly.

"I never thought this would be possible as my trade was so undermanned but, after a few months of talks, I was released from my Avionics Instructor role and moved across to join Force Development Training Squadron. This is where I discovered my calling," she says. Despite being the most junior rank in a small team, Kelly found freedom in her new role that she had never had before. Kelly realised that freedom was exactly what she had been yearning for, although she never expected to encounter that realisation while serving in the military.

"It was during this period of my life I knew my passion lay with helping and empowering others, not fixing aircraft. My days were so varied; some days I was coaching neuro-diverse students and staff, others I was delivering the Human Performance course; some days I was assisting people with force development or team building activities, and others I was organising guest speakers for the staff and students. Every day was so different. Over the next six months I also qualified as a teacher and a mindfulness teacher," says Kelly.

On completion of her mindfulness training, Kelly created and delivered a mindfulness course for the MOD and it was here that things really started to fall into place. "I realised that our business post the RAF would be based around wellbeing and promoting positive mental health," says Kelly. "Jamie and I also qualified as First Aid for Mental Health instructors in our final few months of service. We were both content that we had gained the necessary qualifications and experience to confidently launch a business in our chosen field."

Now Kelly and Jamie run YourNorth, a mental wellbeing training and coaching company. YourNorth delivers accredited First Aid for Mental Health training; accredited Safeguarding courses; wellbeing masterclasses including happiness and kindness, managing stress, and goal setting; mental wellbeing coaching; personal development coaching; mindfulness; and hypnotherapy. "Wellbeing is promoted and developed across all aspects of the training and coaching we provide," says Kelly.

"We discuss the benefits of looking after our wellbeing and the effect it has on our mental health when we deliver First Aid for Mental Health courses, and also when we deliver our wellbeing masterclasses. Ascertaining a coaching client's level of wellbeing is super important as more often than not, the reason they come for coaching is not usually the reason or limiting belief they are presenting," says Kelly. "We are regularly approached by a business group that we are associated with called Welsh ICE, to create and deliver workshops covering topics such as stress and resilience, and mindfulness and mental health. We are also regularly contacted by people who require signposting to other professional agencies."

In addition to the formal training they offer, YourNorth are very active on social media, and the majority of their posts are based around providing valuable wellbeing content. They also run a Facebook community group associated with the YourNorth business page, called MyNorth. This community group promotes positive mental health and wellbeing, and the members are encouraged to post funny and uplifting content, and share their wins, big and small. This community has been nurtured as a safe space, so members feel confident to reach out for help, should they need it.

"We launched YourNorth in March 2020 during the first Covid-19 lockdown. Who launches a face-to-face training company during a pandemic?! Anyway, we did and even though we had to go back to the drawing board almost immediately to redefine our business, we knew the value of what we had to offer, especially during the challenging times we found ourselves in," says Kelly. "We have been delivering our services online throughout the pandemic and were very excited to head back into the classroom in June 2021. Looking back on our first year in business, we are so proud of what we have achieved and how many people we have helped, either directly through our training and coaching or through the information we are pushing out on our social accounts."

Kelly believes that self-awareness is the key to improving wellbeing; that how aware a person is of how they think, feel, and behave will determine how open they are to change. "I encourage everyone to develop a growth mindset and to become open to exploring a different approach to areas of their lives that can be improved. Many people adopt an attitude of 'I've always been like this' and potentially label themselves. This fixed mindset is a barrier and a limiting belief, and this can be challenged through gentle, yet effective, questioning and by encouraging curiosity," she says.

"In an ideal world, prevention is better than correction so if someone can incorporate techniques into their daily lives to build resilience, they will be better equipped to deal with the inevitable ups and downs of life. However, depending on what the client discloses to me about their presenting signs and symptoms will determine the specific advice I offer. For example, if someone tells me they have a suspected mental health condition, I will always recommend they speak with a healthcare professional or contact a relevant professional agency."

For those looking to generally improve their wellbeing, Kelly's advice would be dependent on the area they wanted to work on. "For physical health, drink plenty of water and eat nutritious food. Keep active and move every day, if possible. Be mindful of using drugs or alcohol as coping mechanisms or to aid sleep. Keep on top of personal hygiene," she says. Kelly also recommends spending time in nature, going outside, and getting fresh air and vitamin D. If this is not possible, then sitting by the window, having indoor plants, and being around animals are also wonderful for improving wellbeing.

"If sleep is an issue, consider implementing a routine to wind down before bedtime. This will involve avoiding phone and computer screens for about an hour before bed," says Kelly. "Do something relaxing like have a bath, ensure your bedroom is comfortable and a cool temperature. Binaural beats are fab to assist sleep as the frequency is engineered to slow down brain waves. Lavender essential oil on your pillow is also really helpful."

Creativity is another of Kelly's recommendations. "There are plenty of in-person and online groups offering a diverse range of activities. Crafting is a fantastic and a wonderful way to introduce mindfulness into an activity. Take up a new hobby or revisit a hobby you used to enjoy but for some reason stopped doing. Physical self-care such as yoga, sleep, stretching; emotional self-care like journaling, stress management, and compassion; and social self-care such as personal boundaries or ending toxic relationships, are all examples of ways you can improve your wellbeing," she says.

Building on this, nurturing relationships are so important for wellbeing. Kelly suggests reaching out to friends and family by phone or video message, especially if you are unable to meet in person. You could write a letter to someone you have not spoken to in a while, or alternatively, you could reach out to a support group or volunteer to befriend others who are feeling isolated. This is particularly important whilst working from home. Create a support committee within your place of work or, if you are self-employed, join a networking group or connect with like-minded professionals.

"Whilst working from home, remember to establish a workday routine and have a dedicated area for a productive work environment. Find a balanced approach to work," says Kelly. "Stress management techniques such as breathwork, exercise, sleep, meditation, journaling, grounding techniques, mood tracker apps, listening to music, and Epsom bath salts, which increase magnesium levels and reduce stress hormones, are useful in this area."

Kelly's next tip is around mindfulness. "This allows us to remain in the present, observing our thoughts and feelings without judgement. Anxiety is future-based, therefore, mindfulness is especially effective here as if we are in the present, we cannot be worrying about the 'what next?' and 'what if?'", she says. "Being mindful of how we speak to ourselves is paramount for our wellbeing. If your self-talk is negative, write down the opposite of what you are saying and repeat this mantra throughout the day. If you find yourself over-apologising when you have not done anything wrong, I invite you to reframe 'I'm sorry' with 'thank you'- for example, 'thank you for your patience with my reply'."

Finally, gratitude. "Gratitude is the secret weapon in the quest for improved wellbeing. Especially during the challenging times we have found ourselves living in, it is important we focus on what we do have rather than what we do not have. Gratitude releases dopamine, which is the brain's 'reward centre', and the more we are grateful for, the more we find to be grateful for. You can express and practice gratitude through journaling, telling people, writing letters, popping notes in a gratitude jar or keeping a pleasant events diary," says Kelly.

YourNorth is not the only company in here to be run by former uniformed service staff turned coaches. Robyn Ramsell was a Police Officer before she became a Trauma and Loss Coach, and now uses that experience to support other emergency service personnel and first responders. Robyn is also an advocate for mental strength and wellbeing, and uses a pragmatic and practical approach to help clients develop personal strategies to manage their situation and move on with their futures.

"My career as a Police Officer was not extraordinary, it was everyday policing. There were some major incidents, but the problem for me was not having the strategies to process what I was facing; in essence, I did not know how to look after my own mental wellbeing," says Robyn. "In the end, it cost me my career and I chose to leave a job I loved because I needed to put myself and my family first. I had to understand and acknowledge that I had been living in my survival self and blocking out my feelings. I had unconsciously built a complex defence system. I was not in tune with my body or mind; I was numb to life."

After leaving the role, Robyn went through traditional therapy routes like counselling and psychotherapy. While she describes these as being fantastic, Robyn felt she needed more. "I wanted robust strategies for managing what happens in life. I have learnt that we cannot remove trauma and loss from our lives, but we can develop strategies to move beyond them. I spent a long time going over what I had seen and experienced, which was helpful for a time, but I needed to find a way to break the cycle," she says.

In 2020, Robyn lost an ex-colleague and friend to suicide and this prompted her move towards setting up her own coaching business. "I decided I could not sit back and read about the mental health crisis affecting our emergency services anymore, and I wanted to be a part of the solution," she says. "I think we put too much emphasis on crisis intervention. By the time someone is in crisis the personal cost to them and those around them is extensive. But mental fitness will not just happen. We need to work on it as we do with our physical fitness, and it needs to be maintained."

In order to help with the ongoing maintenance, which is so important for mental wellbeing, Robyn starts by working with her clients on increasing their self-awareness. "It is key for them to recognise in themselves how they really are before they get into crisis, and to have the confidence to seek help. The focus is on moving forward, it is giving people the tools and strategies they need to process what has happened and build personal resilience for what is to come. Particularly in the emergency services you will hear people say, "it's just a job", but it is not just a job, it is an extraordinary job done by extraordinary people who need to be able to protect their mental wellbeing to enable them to move forward and face life with confidence and inner strength," she says.

"I would say every single person has the power within them to take positive control of their own mental wellbeing. It is about finding the right person for you to work with. Needing someone's help is not a weakness; I believe it shows great self-awareness and strength. There are so many other options out there in addition to traditional therapies. Just because your GP or occupational health service offer counselling, it does not mean you cannot take control of your own journey. For me and my recovery, coaching was the turning point where I really started to move forward and that is why I do it now."

Education is also hugely important for supporting and promoting mental wellbeing as Recreate-U CEO Claire Benson and Director Jennie Hughes know all too well. After noticing increasing stress levels among her students, experienced teacher Claire founded children's wellbeing business Calm Children in 2012. Meanwhile, Jennie had started writing educational articles for a parenting website alongside her work in education. Trying to explain parenthesis to bewildered parents in under 400 words lead her to realise just how high curriculum requirements are now compared to 'when we were at school'.

"Watching the effects of the Covid-19 pandemic on the children we work with, we realised that educational attainment and wellbeing are inextricably linked," they say. "Stressed-out people struggle with work, and feeling like you're not doing well creates stress. We saw the need for support which could address both, so we founded Recreate-U to offer bespoke services tailored to the needs of individual children and families."

Recreate-U is a Community Interest Company based on over 30 years of combined teaching experience throughout Greater Manchester and abroad. "Our passion is helping people learn and grow so they can achieve their full potential. We offer specialist support to schools, families, and communities, with services that are carefully designed to include each of the five areas of wellbeing. From stress-busting mindfulness sessions to language courses for lifelong learning or nature walks to get people moving, we offer people the opportunity to find something that works for them," they say.

"Our work with children in particular will help the next generation to understand how to support their own wellbeing. Children who learn early on to understand their mental health are more likely to develop into resilient adults who can then pass on these tools to children in their own lives. Our Calm sessions use a combination of neuroscience, mindfulness, and relaxation techniques to explain how our brains work and what we can do to support our own wellbeing. This compliments our other offers such as tutoring support and hobby sessions. We also offer support and tips via our social media."

For Claire and Jennie, wellbeing means having a life that works for you and meets your needs. They know that this will look different for everyone as everyone thrives on different things. The most important part though is to be honest with yourself and reach out for help if you need it. The Recreate-U team have also come up with a number of hints and tips to help with improving wellbeing, and it all starts with doing a genuine assessment on life as it is right now.

"The chapter headings of this book would be a great place to start. Under each title, write down what is working, what is not working, what makes you light up, and what makes you shrink down. This might feel scary at first, but it is only an audit. You do not need to act on it unless you want to," they say. "Remember, this is not an audit of how well you have met society's expectations. This is an audit of how happy your life is making you."

While this is a deeply personal activity, it can also stay private. "No one else needs to see it, so no dodging the big stuff. You cannot change what you will not admit to. All the bubble baths in the world are not going to help that much if what is really making you miserable is the fact that you spend 40 hours a week doing something you hate, or that you have no time for hobbies because your partner refuses to take their turn doing the housework. So be honest," say Claire and Jennie.

"Once you have worked out which areas of your life need work and which are working pretty well already, it is time to make a plan. Again, everyone's needs are different, which is a good thing because it means shorter queues for whatever you are after. Although we have divided life into different areas to work out a wellbeing action plan, it is important to remember that our lives do not fit into watertight compartments. This can be a plus or a minus depending on how you look at it."

This echoes the concept behind this book, that everything is connected. "One difficult experience can have knock-on effects in all areas of your life and wellbeing. On the other hand, so can a good one. Especially if you are short on time, that is good news because it means you can tackle two goals at once. One of our biggest recommendations for improving wellbeing is spending time in nature, so let us use that as an example," they say.

"If you have decided to get more exercise from your audit, try planning a hike or some canoeing over the weekend. If you have written down 'give back to the community' or 'make more friends' in your life audit, look into outdoor volunteering opportunities. If your problem is feeling bored and uninspired, why not try a new outdoor sport like geocaching or surfing? Of course, it does not need to be something big like this to be useful."

The Recreate-U Team also suggest that even just sitting in a local park for ten or twenty minutes can bring huge benefits. Combining this with relaxation or mindfulness exercises can really help blow the stress away. And if you are not sure what to do, there are some free resources on the Recreate-U website. If you do not have access to outside space, try getting some houseplants, some living herbs from the supermarket, or even growing some seedlings in a window box. Not only will you get tasty vegetables or pretty flowers but nourishing another living thing has also been proven to increase wellbeing.

Having a support network is another huge influence on wellbeing. "The impact of loneliness on mental health is only just beginning to be understood, and it is already proven to significantly affect wellbeing," says Claire and Jennie. "When you have been socially isolated, problems can start to seem much more overwhelming than they really are. If you have found yourself isolated, for example because friends have moved away, reaching out to local community groups and services or signing up to volunteer and give something back to your community can be a great place to start making connections."

Claire and Jennie understand that sometimes making improvements can feel overwhelming. "A life is a big thing to change; after all, it has taken you all the time you have been here to end up where you are now. It is a bit like steering the Titanic, sometimes you can say 'change', but it might take a while to gather the momentum to go in a new direction. Learning to create the life you want takes time, especially if you have gone through some tough experiences in the past. Just like we did not learn to walk overnight, it might take a few tries, falls and even crying sessions before we see the results we are after," they say.

Our brains remember things, so we have shortcuts when we meet a similar situation in the future. This means that old thoughts and patterns of behaviour tend to stick around long after they have outlived their usefulness. We need to give our minds a spring clean from time to time. In the sessions by Recreate-U they call this 'taking the thought to court'. This works like putting the old thought up on the stand and cross-examining it like a witness in a television courtroom drama. If it cannot prove it is both true and useful, it does not belong.

"Now we have let you know about the hard parts, it is time for some positivity," says Claire and Jennie. "The good news is that taking even tiny steps towards improving your wellbeing is likely to bring benefits in terms of mental health. That is because one of the really key elements of wellbeing is a sense of agency. Feeling powerless is one of the biggest sources of stress around, and with everything going on in the world, it is easy to feel that improving your life is beyond your control."

Their advice here is to 'look for the cracks'. "What we mean by that is there is always something you can do, even if it is tiny. Like a rock climber scaling a seemingly impassable cliff face, you will always get at least a little finger-hold somewhere, even if it is somewhere awkward, unexpected, and mildly terrifying. But seriously, even something as simple as a phone call to a friend, searching for information online, or emailing a local service like ours can offer that all-important sense of being able to do something about it," they say.

"Of course, there is far more we could say. But if we had to condense our wellbeing philosophy down to a few sentences, we would say this: do the things that make you light up, reach out for help when you need it, and even the tiniest step in the right direction counts."

Chapter summary

My personal experience has taught me how much of an impact poor mental health and wellbeing can have on life as a whole. It can be scary, dark, and lonely, and it is understandable that sometimes people can see no way out. But if that experience has taught me anything, it is that it can and will get better, you just have to keep going, one day at a time, one step at a time, one breath at a time. Therefore, the information, advice, and guidance in this chapter really resonates with me; especially the following three things:

Firstly, education, training, and awareness are absolutely essential. The more we can engage people in discussions around this topic, the less taboo it will become. Now, I do not believe this is necessarily about teaching what mental health issues look like, but more about teaching what good mental health, wellbeing, self-care, and resilience are, so that they become the focus. It is important to have an understanding of how to recognise illness and crisis, but we should be aiming for the good rather than living in fear of the bad.

Secondly, the younger we can do this, the better. Initiatives are appearing all the time which teach children about mental wellbeing and engage them in activities that include nature, outdoor spaces, plants, animals, and all the other good stuff. I'm hopeful these will increase and get better, especially following the Covid-19 pandemic. The world needs resilient adults, and this starts with ensuring our future generations are physically, mentally, and emotionally well.

Thirdly and finally, learning and healing happens in all kinds of ways through all kinds of support. 'Therapy' is a personal and very relational thing so if I could give you one piece of advice, it is to have the courage to seek what is best for you and to challenge what is not. If you are referred to someone that you do not click with, request someone else. Similarly, make the most of chemistry or taster sessions. You are not going to make progress if you cannot trust and open up to someone, so make sure they are a good fit.

In this chapter you have heard from...

Name: Kelly Farr
Name of company: YourNorth
Position in company / Job title: Co-Founder / Mental Wellbeing Trainer & Coach
Company website: www.yournorth.co.uk
Facebook: @YourNorthUK
Twitter: @YourNorth_
Instagram: @YourNorth
LinkedIn: Kelly L Farr

Name: Robyn Ramsell
Name of company: Robyn Ramsell Coaching
Position in company / Job title: Trauma and Loss Coach
Company website: www.robynramsell.co.uk
Instagram: @robynramsellcoaching
LinkedIn: https://www.linkedin.com/in/robyn-ramsell-4614b7181/

Name: Claire Benson and Jennie Hughes
Name of company: Recreate-U
Position in company / Job title: Claire Benson: CEO, Jennie Hughes: Director
Company website: www.recreate-u.co.uk
Facebook: @R3createU
Instagram: @recreate__u
LinkedIn: https://www.linkedin.com/company/Recreate-U
Twitter: @recreate__u

CHAPTER FIVE

Emotional Wellbeing

"Wellness starts from within. If we want to connect to others on an authentic level, it helps to be connected to ourselves first," says Emotional Health Coach Amanda Green. Amanda helps people work with their emotional energy to shift the blocks that are holding them back from their full potential. "I empower people on their journey of transformation and personal leadership through one-to-one coaching and group sessions," she says.

"After working for many years in sales and business development, and training others in sales, I realised that many people struggled with confidence and self-belief and that inspired me to follow my dream of being a coach. I chose to study for a Performance Coaching Diploma. I always knew I loved coaching and empowering people, but I did not have a niche at the time. I then personally had some strong experiences with anxiety which took me on a journey of self-discovery where I learned about emotions, the subconscious, the brain, and spiritual transformation."

With knowledge and experience came a real inspiration to help people with similar struggles. "My work has evolved so much in the past couple of years to a place I could not have imagined. I have transformed my thinking and consciousness, and now I have a unique business. I have the honour and privilege of empowering people to see the truth, to align the soul and ego, to change their perspective of life and of themselves, and become the fullest expression of who they were really meant to be," says Amanda.

"What really lead me into this role was being able to see my life from a soul perspective rather than the wounded ego version, to follow my heart and true passion, to live my truth despite the many fears I had." Amanda uses this same deep level thinking with her clients, helping them to understand that they are divinely destined for their experiences, to connect with their emotional guidance system and understand what it is communicating to them, and to help them to also see life from a soul perspective.

Amanda says this work provides peace, compassion, a zest for life, much better coping and communication skills, and stronger and more enjoyable relationships in all areas of life. "It also helps people move closer to their destiny," she says. "When one person raises their vibration, this impacts everyone around them and their environment. It is like the domino effect. It starts within, then it impacts relationships, environment, community, culture, the world."

Having worked with directors and business owners who have a significant impact on company environments and cultures, Amanda has seen this new perspective impact teams which in turn has influenced families. "We can all make a difference, and it starts with us," she says. Amanda has also offered a few tips on how we can begin to work on ourselves in this way.

"Be prepared to get honest with yourself and find the right support that you resonate with. It is not easy to look at who we really are, but when we can know ourselves very deeply, there is so much good that can happen," she says. "Emotions give us so many clues, but we often see things from a wounded ego perspective and that is generally not conducive to change or transformation. If we want a different result, as Albert Einstein said, we cannot rely on the same level of thinking that got us into the problem in the first place; so, try something different."

One thing people can start doing right now is being more aware and that requires tuning in to your emotions. We can become more aware by paying greater attention to our emotional and physical reactions to people and situations in our lives. "Notice what triggers you or changes your state. Notice when you feel something in your body, perhaps a reaction from the gut or a panicky feeling like a tightness in the chest. Notice feelings of envy, guilt, shame, anger, or not feeling good enough. Also pay attention to the inner dialogue running with this; it will be happening. See if you can be non-judgmental about it all and approach it with an open-minded air of curiosity. Learn what messages you are being given. This is powerful," says Amanda.

Awareness is the key to personal leadership as well as wellbeing and emotional health, according to Vicky Bennett, Chief Executive of HorseHeard, who uses relationship with horses to stimulate wellness and emotional health amongst children, young people, and adults. "Most of the time we are not fully present to our patterns of habit and response. When a person is in the presence of a one-ton horse though, they naturally engage their awareness," she says.

Prior to joining the charity, Vicky spent her life bringing diverse groups of individuals together to create a change in behaviour towards the environment. She found that the most successful solutions were created when individuals valued listening over speaking, cooperation over winning, and quality of living over quantity. The solutions were achieved by individuals stepping beyond their internal patterns, biases, and habits to create something new. It might sound easy but owning your identity with clarity, integrity, and conviction seems to be the hardest thing to achieve.

"That is until you engage with a horse," says Vicky. "I have been privileged enough to witness the journey individuals take with horses, and the power that is enabled when new ways of being are accessed and old patterns changed, allowing life to become a more fulfilling adventure. Horses are highly attuned to their surroundings and they sense and respond to subtle cues in our behaviour. This provides instant and honest feedback, creating experiences which get to the core of issues quickly, powerfully, and effectively."

The experienced and compassionate team at HorseHeard use the horses to help build confidence and self-esteem, to overcome fears, achieve goals, and improve the lives of the people they work with. However, to be clear though, being with the horse does not involve horse riding or horse handling skills. It is about working with groups or individuals and empowering them to produce effective solutions to life's dilemmas and challenges; it is also about helping them to understand and manage who they are.

"Being aware of your role in your own world enables you to explore, let go of what is not serving you, centre new ways of seeing, and gain new insight, wellness, and emotional health. Time with the horses enables people to open their view on their world, to perform better, and to better serve the needs of themselves and those around them. The first step is to ask or reach out for help. In doing so you enable a new path to unfold, you take a step away from where you presently stand and move forward," says Vicky.

"It is very difficult to see yourself, your habits and your 'blind spots'. Blind spots are our inability to understand how our own perceptions skew the way we see the world and how we impact others. Managing your world without having full awareness of your blind spots can limit your ability to move ahead and resolve problems. That is why asking for help is the first step. If that step is in the direction of HorseHeard, we would love to greet you. If you take a step towards another support body, then that is a success too. Only you know which step you will take; the key is to take it."

Our next contributor in the area of emotional wellbeing is Amanda Englishby, a highly established and accredited Coach, Neurolinguistic Programming (NLP) and Emotional Freedom Technique (EFT) Practitioner, writer, and motivational speaker who offers coaching one-to-one and group sessions across the globe, in person, online, or by phone. She is also the resident wellbeing coach for a number of private and corporate companies across the Northwest and she delivers a wide range of wellbeing workshops.

"I identify any problems and/or limiting beliefs which are holding my clients back. I work through a range of varied tools and techniques to help them to move forward and reach their personal and professional goals," she says. "My unique person-centred approach fused with a genuine passion and desire to help others is reflected in the amazing results of my clients and in the testimonies and reviews I receive."

Amanda enjoyed a rewarding thirteen-year career as a teacher and trainer before becoming a coach. "I thrived on helping others to discover their potential and to achieve their goals. I have many fond memories of my students, and their personal and academic development. However, having experienced my own adversities throughout life and possessing a high level of emotional intelligence, my interest in helping others naturally never stopped when the school bell rang. It was this awareness which led me to my own exploration of self-discovery and an interest in understanding the mind," she says.

This was not an easy feat and it took Amanda years of training, working with different analysts, exploring varied forms of alternative therapy, and taking herself away on a year's sabbatical in Australia, New Zealand, and Bali. Upon her return to the UK, and following further training, she now had the evidence that her tools and techniques worked, and that the experiences she had engaged with, studied, and practiced were worthwhile.

"I felt it was such a waste to have all this knowledge and not be able to share it to help others. Therefore, I chose to leave the teaching profession to establish my own business as a Life Coach, NLP, and EFT Practitioner. It is my life experiences and challenges which enable me to empathise with my clients, show compassion, and inspire them to know that change is possible. I have made it my life's purpose to empower people to make the changes they need to live the life they deserve," says Amanda.

The aims of Amanda's coaching practice are to: increase a client's level of happiness; improve and manage their emotional health and mental wellbeing; and encourage a strong, positive, and resilient mindset. These, in turn, create an overall sense of wellbeing and instil people's passion and purpose in life. "Life really is too short to be unhappy," she says. "My main aim is always to honour the past whilst moving people forward and to focus on achievement. Inevitably getting my clients to where they want to be and not keeping them where they were or are."

Describing her coaching style as very eclectic within the scope of tools and techniques she is able to work with, Amanda recognises that no two clients are the same. "We all have our own stories, history, and experience of life, and therefore, will naturally respond differently to the strategies explored. This is always honoured and encompassed throughout all sessions. My clients communicate their goals and desires and I help them to achieve these by shedding any limitations holding them back and working through the emotions involved," she says.

The workshops currently being delivered by Amanda are as follows: how to manage stress; how to manage anxiety; how to build resilience; how to set and achieve goals; how to build and maintain a positive mindset; how to find you again; and the law of attraction. This list is not exhaustive and Amanda will often devise alternative workshops based on the needs of the community, setting, and organisation.

"Due to the current pressured society we live in today, a lot of people are struggling with high levels of stress and anxiety. I see this in my daily practice and when working with my partner organisations. Before going any further, it is important to note the difference between these two terms. They, unfortunately, are often used interchangeably, when in actual fact they are two very different conditions," says Amanda.

"Stress, unlike anxiety, is a response to an inappropriate level of daily pressures. Pressures such as: a change in career, study, workload, family, finances, relationships, and traumatic events like death, divorce, abuse, and injury. We can usually identify which area of our life is causing the stress level to increase and address it. Anxiety is different. It can be triggered by stress, though there is not always an identifiable root cause. It can often be an overwhelming feeling of dread or an irrational fear of the future. The feeling of anxiety will often not dissipate once the cause of the stressful situation has passed."

If both conditions are prolonged and not managed in the interim stages, they can have a hugely detrimental effect on our emotional health and mental wellbeing: high blood pressure; increased levels of adrenaline and cortisol; headaches; lack of sleep; irritability; low mood; constant worry; lack of concentration; and a change in appetite, as examples. If experienced over a sustained period of time, these can lead to chronic stress and/or an anxiety disorder.

"EFT and NLP are both highly effective techniques to help lessen levels of stress and anxiety. Though for the purposes of this book, here are some practical tools and tips which you may wish to explore. The first is to take a bird's eye view on the different areas of your life: family, fun and social activities, business or career, personal growth, technology and social media, and health. Now explore how much time and energy you currently dedicate to each. This may give you an idea of what is currently out of balance and what might be causing you stress," says Amanda.

"Next is to practice simple breathing exercises whenever the initial feeling arises. Use these as soon as you feel the sensation in your body; do not wait until the feeling gets more intense or further worrying thoughts start to form. There are many breathing exercises you can explore and follow on the internet or via an App. However, a simple one that my clients find greatly effective is 'square breathing'. People enjoy this particular exercise as it is easy to remember and can be practised almost anywhere."

"Start by taking a few breaths in and out first. In through the nose and out through the mouth. Then, visualise a square. Starting in the bottom left-hand corner, breathe in as you count to four moving up the side of the square. Hold your breath for four counts along the top of the square. Breathe out for four as you go down the right side of the square. Then hold your breath for four as you go along the baseline back to the starting position. You simply repeat this until your heart rate and blood pressure have lowered, then you can think with more clarity and manage the emotion," she says.

Amanda teaches that breathing exercises help to provide the space between the thought and the connected feeling or emotion, and in turn, stop the level of intensity increasing. "Daily meditation practice will also help to build inner calm and a peaceful state of mind. This means that when events, experiences, or thoughts arise which may trigger anxiety or stress, we are able to manage and move through them rather than freeze, react, or run," she says.

"You do not have to meditate for an hour a day cross-legged on a mat. If you can, that is great, but if not, that is fine too. The amount of time you dedicate to the meditation practice should be realistic for your lifestyle. For some people, this is ten minutes a day sat on the side of their bed, for others it is an hour or more. You should certainly feel the benefits from ten minutes a day and there are plenty of guided meditations you can try out online or via meditation apps."

The third is to keep active to raise your 'happy hormones': dopamine, endorphins, and serotonin. "This in turn will help boost and regulate your mood, providing you with a sense of wellness and fulfilment. Again, do what works for you, whether that is 20 minutes or an hour of walking, gym workouts, yoga, football, rugby, dancing, cycling; whichever activity you enjoy most. Similarly, try to make more time for your outlets and plan fulfilling activities. Ask yourself what did you used to enjoy that you do not do anymore? Reading, watching movies, art, connecting with others?" says Amanda.

Spending time with other people can keep your spirits high and maintain avenues of support. Amanda recommends trying to plan this in each week: a coffee, a walk or even a phone or video call if distance is a problem. Make the effort and do not wait for someone else to make the invitation. Also, try to ensure you are getting enough sleep by creating a dedicated night-time routine which helps your body and brain to switch off and relax before bed. For example, turn your phone onto airplane mode to resist checking emails or social media, have a bath, read, meditate, journal, or dim the lights. Again, create a routine that works for you and your lifestyle.

Next, Amanda says to eat nourishing food at regular intervals throughout the day to feed not only the body but the brain too. "There is a reason the term 'hangry' was created. If you are not eating regularly, your cortisol and adrenaline levels will increase and feelings of stress, anxiety, and at times, even anger might arise. Ensure you are including a mix of proteins, vegetables, and complex carbs in your daily meals and having regular nourishing snacks to keep hunger at bay, and manage your mood and emotions," she says.

"Finally, avoid too much sugar and caffeine. Although both may give you a short-term boost of energy, when they wear off, it can cause your mood and energy to decrease, and your cortisol level to rise, therefore, exacerbating feelings of anxiety and stress. Try to stick to decaf after lunch and monitor your sugar intake. If you have been or are struggling with stress or anxiety, I hope you find benefit from the strategies provided above. Although, like anything in life, to see the results you have to put in the practice."

With any emotion or feeling we experience, it should be honoured and explored. "They are often a signal that something needs to change or be worked through. Inevitably this helps us to take action and live the life we deserve. I have many more techniques to help within this area. I also have specialised techniques to address any underlying problems or beliefs which may be causing the stress or anxiety to continue. Therefore, please feel free to make contact if you or your organisation require further support," says Amanda.

A barrister turned trauma-informed therapist Lisa Shannon struggled with crippling depression for more than 30 years. "Feeling broken, I was constantly angry and frustrated, reacting to every trigger, it was exhausting for me and my family. Always searching for a cure, I trained in counselling, Cognitive Behavioural Therapy and NLP. While they all helped, they did not cure me. Instead, they added fuel to my belief that I was too broken to be fixed. When I hit midlife, things got really serious with 3 thwarted suicide attempts in 16 days. But somewhere, hidden deep in the back of my mind was a niggle that maybe, I had a purpose," she says.

"Yet I knew that if I was to stay alive, drastic action was needed, no one was coming to save me. And so, my healing journey began. Very quickly I realised that I was not broken at all, I had experienced immense childhood trauma that could be repaired. After healing the emotional wounds, abandoning my out-dated beliefs and rehabilitating my mindset, I was transformed. Feeling, thinking and believing entirely different things about yourself changes your world, the people in it, and your aspirations." Lisa now lives the life that she grew up believing was not available to her.

"With complete trust in my intuition, I trained as a hypnotherapist and, combined with my existing skills, I have founded a unique programme which helps others to transform too. Without doubt, this is my life's purpose. My practice is centred on early childhood experiences because that is where the blueprint for how we feel about ourselves originates. Usually buried deep in our subconscious, the symptoms of unhelpful childhood experiences continue to show up in our everyday lives until we become aware of them. Usually presenting as emotions such as anger, frustration and hopelessness," she says.

"Our early experiences are so significant because as children, we quickly learn that we must like what others like to fit in and be accepted. From an early age we bend and shape ourselves to please others, becoming who they want us to be, so never actually learning who we really are. Understanding and getting to know ourselves is crucial to our wellbeing and is fundamental to being able to establish healthy boundaries, trust, and compassion. It is these skills that help us to keep well, to thrive, and to self soothe in trying times."

Being able to self soothe is a vital component for building resilience, and allows us to deal with our emotions quickly and more rationally. For some, these vital skills were taught and encouraged in childhood, for many they were not. This can happen for a number of reasons but primarily, it is because parents were not taught the skills either. Fortunately, these fundamental skills can be learned in adulthood and the starting point is getting to know yourself. One of the best ways to begin is by checking how you are actually feeling.

"Many of us are acutely aware of the symptoms that our feelings can create such as shouting, hitting out, and temper tantrums, but not of the feelings themselves. By spending time getting to understand how you are truly feeling, you will begin to have some insight into what you really like, what you are comfortable with, and what actually matters to you. Naturally, it will also draw attention to areas that may be problematic, but once you become aware you can start to make changes. As you do this checking, you will become conscious of situations that trigger an emotional response. This is often because of an unhelpful belief that you have," says Lisa.

"Our beliefs are formed as a result of our early childhood experiences, usually before the age of seven. This is because before then, we have limited cognitive reasoning and our minds are like sponges to the messages that we are exposed to. We look to the adults that surround us for guidance on how to feel about ourselves and how to view the world; we believe everything they tell us as we rely on them to look after us and keep us safe. However, many adults have unhelpful childhood beliefs too and this forms a 'generational wound' that gets passed on from generation to generation comprising of their version of who you 'should' be, what you should do, and how you should act."

Doing this work is an exciting opportunity to heal your wounds and liberate the next generation from the limits these beliefs impose. Unhelpful beliefs are usually attached to a memory which creates feelings that in turn cause concern around the behaviour they provoke. Angry outbursts or tearful episodes associated with anger and hopelessness can make relationships difficult, this behaviour is what usually has people seeking help. While anger itself is a feeling just like any other, it can be problematic if not handled in a safe way. Connecting and getting to know these triggers will help you to identify the belief which you can then work on updating, because they are very rarely true. It is more likely that they reflect the beliefs of your early caregivers.

"Writing down your uncensored feelings allows you to express them safely while gaining great insight. Stay with the inquiry and write what you are truly feeling and why, allow the words to flow. Doing this, particularly for situations that have triggered behaviour that causes you issues, will help you to find the memory and unhelpful belief attached. Then you can reframe the belief from the point of view of your adult self, no longer reliant on the opinion of others. The only opinion that matters now is yours, and you can decide to change that anytime you choose," says Lisa.

Lisa believes that learning about yourself on this deeper level and understanding what matters to you is a gateway to learning the other crucial skills for your wellbeing. "Knowing what you like, you will begin to trust yourself and understand what brings you comfort, you will also find it easier to self-soothe. Recognising what matters, will enable you to establish healthy boundaries and feel comfortable protecting them. Understanding your story allows you to exercise self-compassion and celebrate your journey. It also gives you the power to make the changes you need to make, to be who you want to be," she says.

Chapter summary

As a highly empathic and sensitive individual, I am no stranger to fluctuations in my own emotions and those of people around me. I like a good cry, and this can be triggered by anything from a birthday card to a soppy film, a tragic news report to pretty much anything to do with animals. I am used to it now and often must put boundaries in place around what I am exposed to, so I do not get overwhelmed. There are some key pieces of advice in this chapter though:

The first is that emotional honesty is the foundation of emotional wellbeing. Until we get to grips with what is really going on and why, we cannot make any positive changes. Instead, we remain stuck in our patterns and habits which ultimately hold us back. By exploring, understanding, and healing our own emotional wounds we are less likely to be angered, frustrated, or upset by events around us. On top of that, we will be more emotionally available for the other people in our lives.

The second is that support for emotional wellbeing can come in all shapes, sizes, and forms, so do not rule anything out.

The third and final, is understanding the impact of stress and anxiety on our emotions, and finding the tools, tips, tricks, and techniques to manage the levels of stress and anxiety in our lives. These will ultimately help us to maintain healthy levels of emotional wellness, to respond and not react, and to be able to pass them on to others who might be in distress.

In this chapter you have heard from...

Name: Amanda Green
Name of company: Amanda Green Coaching
Position in company / Job title: Emotional Health Coach
Company website: www.amandagreencoaching.co.uk
Facebook: @amandagreencoaching
Instagram: @amandagreenemotionalhealthcoach
Twitter: @actualisecoach

Name: Vicky Bennett
Name of company: HorseHeard
Position in company / Job title: Chief Executive
Company website: HorseHeard.com
Facebook: @HorseHeard
Twitter: @HorseHeard

Name: Amanda Englishby
Name of company: Amanda Englishby Ltd
Position in company / Job title: CEO
Company website: www.amandaenglishby.co.uk
Facebook: @Amandaenglishbycoaching
LinkedIn: amanda-englishby-659850127/
Instagram: @aenglishbycoaching

Name: Lisa Shannon
Name of company: Lisa Shannon
Position in company or Job title: Trauma Informed Advanced Hypnotherapist
Company website: http://lisashannon.co.uk/
Facebook: @lisa.shannon.378
LinkedIn: lisa-shannon-rtt/
Instagram: @lisa.v.shannon

PART TWO

Connection to Others

CHAPTER SIX

Relational Wellbeing

The 75-year Grant Study from Yale University concluded that the key indicator to the quality of life is the quality of your personal relationships. They are fundamental to the long-term happiness, fulfilment, and overall wellbeing that someone will experience throughout their lives, and John Kenny, The Relationship Guy, helps people to create that quality. As a coach to women who want to get into a healthy intimate relationship, John helps them understand the main reasons why people attract certain types of relationships into their lives and the subsequent impacts these relationships have.

"After I finished my athletic career, I had no idea what I wanted to do with my life. From the age of 18 I had wanted to become a full-time athlete, running for Great Britain on several occasions, but I had never reached the level that meant I could do it for a living. I decided to try teaching and went back to college, then university. Whilst studying, part of the course was an introduction to counselling and when I decided teaching was not for me, I looked at taking counselling further," says John.

"In the meantime, I had joined the London Fire Brigade and whilst serving there I went to college and took a diploma in therapeutic counselling. After several years of being a therapist, I met a coach and had some sessions with her as she pointed out that I was helping a lot of people in their lives, but mine was still full of issues. Counselling had taught me how to understand myself, but not how to move on and change my life."

John took a diploma in coaching and began to integrate it into his work. He took many other coaching courses too believing, at the time, that having all of the certificates would make him a good coach. He also added a hypnotherapy and psychology diploma. "In 2016, after rupturing my knee ligament and not being able to walk for several weeks, and after giving it a lot of thought, I decided to amalgamate all of my experience and qualifications and formed Interpersonal Relationship Coaching (IRC) to focus on what I was best at, relationships," he says.

"IRC takes the bits from coaching, counselling, psychology, and hypnotherapy that I think are key to understanding why people think, feel, and do as they do, and attract specific types of people into their lives dictating the quality of their relationships," says John. "Having come from a history of toxic and unhealthy relationships of my own I have a deep understanding of the impacts these have and wanted to help people to manage their own difficult relationship spaces. In 2020, I decided that I wanted to help people find the best quality relationships for themselves and The Relationship Guy came into being."

Through his coaching business, John offers 90-day, one-to-one Relationship-Ready packages, and a one-off four-hour Relationship Breakthrough session to individuals who either have a history of difficult or disappointing relationships, have avoided deeper connection as they do not know how to be close to someone, or have focused on becoming a success in another area of life and now want to find that person to complement their lifestyle. When working with individuals, one of the things that John focuses on is their attachment type.

"Attachment is what is used to describe how we learn to connect with others emotionally. A secure attachment style is important for healthy emotional development. A secure attachment is attained when a child is treated with love, support, and encouragement, and healthy bonds are created with their primary caregivers as they grow up. Later-life trauma can have an impact on the security of attachment, even if the early experiences have been positive. Similarly, an unhealthy attachment can be made secure with the awareness of the issue that caused it," says John.

"An insecure attachment, however, can lead to difficulties connecting to people, and therefore, have a long-term detrimental impact on someone's life. An insecure attachment is the likely outcome when a child has been subject to Adverse Childhood Experiences (ACE), such as physical, mental and emotional abuse, neglect, trauma, and household dysfunction. Although it is not one hundred per cent the case. It is all a matter of how a child's brain perceives its environment growing up. When a child is unable to process the pain they are experiencing, their brain will find a way to alleviate this discomfort."

Whichever way the brain manages to do this, it is usually then how the attachment style develops. The types of insecure or disordered attachments are: Anxious, Avoidant, Anxious/Avoidant also known as Disorganised. John explains the three in the following way, "have you ever noticed that some children scream, shout, cry or make some other attempt in order to gain attention? They grab legs or roll on the floor, all to be noticed? They have lost control of their feelings and are looking for someone to placate them, soothe them and generally make them feel at ease. They become very needy and are not able to stop their behaviour until someone steps in to make them feel better," he says.

This is what can be described as an anxious attachment in children. If this continues into adult life, then that person will become anxious when they experience a perceived painful encounter and act out in order to get someone to take away this uncertainty within them. They are unable to self-soothe and make it right within themselves. Someone you may describe as liking a 'bit of drama', clingy, or needy.

"An avoidant personality type however will be the type of child that keeps quiet, goes to be by themselves and is often referred to as the child that does not cause any problems. In this case, they have decided that the best way to manage their painful experiences is to shut it away, comply, and internalise it all," says John. "As an adult, they find it difficult to connect deeply due to the perceived pain of it going wrong and will withdraw before this happens in order to protect themselves. You may see the term 'ghosting' used quite widely and this could be a sign of an avoidant personality."

Someone who has the most extreme unhealthy attachment of anxious/avoidant or disorganised, will more than likely be someone who has experienced severe abuse or trauma in childhood, or occasionally in later life. "This might include physical or sexual abuse, or witnessing traumatic acts carried out by the primary care giver. The outcome of whatever experience is two-fold. The betrayal of safety has occurred and although the child still loves and craves love from this person, they also realise this person can be a serious threat," says John.

"In adult relationships unhealthy attachments play out as a need to connect, to belong, to love and be loved, but also a need to survive and to protect themselves from possible harm. They experience anxiety at the thought of bonding and then avoidance occurs to protect themselves. In a lot of insecure attachments people will struggle with low self-confidence, self-worth, and self-esteem. In extreme cases it can lead to Borderline Personality Disorder, Dependency Disorder, Narcissistic Personality Disorder and Avoidant Personality Disorder."

John also says that people who have an insecure attachment are more prevalent to depression and general anxiety, addiction, eating disorders, and alexithymia (lacking emotional awareness in self and others) but attachment type is not the only factor. Another crucial thing to understand in order to live your best relationships possible are your relationship patterns. The relationships you experience as you grow up leave subconscious markers that your brain remembers and recalls each time you meet someone new in your life. It looks for signs that you are familiar with and has a tendency to move towards what it knows.

"If your relationships have been healthy, then this is obviously a positive thing as your brain will take you towards something good and will be wary of something it does not recognise. However, if your experiences have been negative, then your brain will only recognise these and lead you towards these unhealthy experiences repeatedly. It may know that it is leading you into something that is likely to cause you some sort of pain, but it is a pain that you are used to," says John. "I like to call these 'cotton wool' and 'spikey' relationships. You know that the spikes will hurt you, but you also know you will survive it. The cotton wool can give you all the comfort you need, but as you do not know what it feels like, you avoid it."

John adds that, "when you enter into a relationship, you have an end goal in mind. If, when you were young, your ways of doing relationships were to end up by yourself, away from the people that caused you pain, then as you get older, you look for the same or similar outcomes. To be by yourself was your safe space and your brain will look to find this for you every time. You may therefore find yourself purposefully choosing the same people just because you know where it is going to end," he says.

When you grew up, were love, time, encouragement, compassion, understanding and acceptance given unconditionally? Or were there certain criteria you had to meet? Was it conditional? We develop our relationship beliefs based on this and it is also something that is critical for knowing if you are to develop the great relationships you want in life. We all carry a set of beliefs and they are the most powerful thing you can have in your life. Beliefs are the only thing that override your survival instinct and therefore can dictate the life you live and the relationships you allow in your life.

"If you grew up believing that relationships are difficult, that love and affection are temporary, that the person you love causes you pain, or that you need to be a certain way in order to gain affection, then you will always believe this to be true. Not only that, but you will always be looking for ways to make this true. Your beliefs are your truths. If these truths are not present in your life, if what is happening seems to go against what you believe, then your mind will not feel at ease, it will feel discomfort until you make something happen that you are more comfortable with," says John.

"If you are with someone who shows you they care, makes time for you, and puts in effort for you, but this is something you are not used to, then the likelihood is that you will reject it. Not only will you reject it, but you will do something or convince yourself of something that confirms your belief, your truth, and not allow the relationship to continue. All three things, your attachment style, your relational patterns and your relational beliefs will dictate the types of relationships that you will attract and be attracted to."

According to John, this all comes down to your subconscious. "The energy that you put into fulfilling the subconscious criteria you have set for yourself will also be something that the other person is doing. When you meet you will either have a match made in heaven, or a match made in maladaptive needs that creates an unhealthy, sometimes toxic, and occasionally destructive relationship. But ultimately one that you are choosing whether you realise it or not," he says.

So, if the subconscious plays such a big part in our relationships, how do we go about breaking the cycle? John says that the most important thing you need to do in order to improve your wellbeing in the area of relationships is to get to know you. By understanding yourself, your attachment style, your relational patterns, and your relationship beliefs, will enable you to recognise what you are doing that impacts on your happiness, your fulfilment, your connection to others, the quality of your relationships, and ultimately the quality of your life.

"Do you know what you want in a relationship? Or do you just know what you do not want? If you keep looking for what you do not want then that is always what you will find. There is something called the Reticular Activating System (RAS) which is your 'I will look for what you want or focus on' part of your brain. It specifically looks for what you tell it to look for and, if that is something you do not want, it will find it for you. I like to think of it as the law of attraction and if your brain is stuck on an attachment, outdated beliefs and unhealthy patterns, your RAS will be focused on keeping these going," says John.

"Knowing all of this now I am able to decide what I want for my future relationships; something I had never allowed before. I now focus my RAS only on what I want in life rather than what I do not want. When the old patterns, beliefs and attachment fears kick in, I thank my brain for trying to keep me safe but tell it that this stuff is now out of date, not what I want any longer, and remind it of what I do want now. Can you do the same?"

Lou Chiu, who works in the arena of culture and relationships, is helping organisations cultivate organisational and cultural wellness through training, group facilitation, coaching, and consultancy services. Lou specialises in developing and supporting individuals and communities who want to be confident, informed, and effective allies. "Growing up bilingual, language, culture, and etiquette has been something I have had an interest in. Relationships are key to how we see, interpret, and interact with the world. It is the source of both frustration and joy," she says.

"I believe that we have learned so many ways to communicate that we make the assumptions that people know what we mean. This can be with your loved ones, co-workers, boss, friends, sports team, neighbours, random people on social media, and even with yourself. My previous roles in education and educational charities shared the driver to enable and equip people to reach their aspirations, whether that was secondary school pupils looking at their options, adult learners returning to education, university students shaping the start of their career or as a charity director with four departments, 2000 student staff and 24,000 members."

This also included working with marginalised and under-represented communities. "By the time I was 34, I had my third burnout as an adult. I was fortunate enough to take a career break to heal, reflect, and come up with a new plan. As I re-emerged a recovering workaholic, I set up my mental health advocacy blog, my coaching practice, and began a master's degree. As I started to share my own story and experiences of being a woman of colour with a history of poor mental health, I was overwhelmed by the honesty in the responses that I got," says Lou.

"My business was born from these shared experiences of hardship, discomfort, and optimism that things can change. This is not easy which is why having a helping hand can really make a difference. I use this combination of lived personal and professional experiences, academic curiosity, and values-led drive to help businesses and not-for-profits untangle existing complications in the workplace, manage conflict between personal and professional spaces, and translate the different languages that are used in relationships at work, at home, and with stakeholders."

Lou has found that language barriers are especially true when the difficult conversations around equality, diversity, inclusion, and discrimination emerge. By helping people overcome some of the tensions associated with racism, ageism, ableism, sexism, homophobia, transphobia, religion, politics, and class, communities can be made up of people who can bring their whole selves because they feel safe, respected, and like they can contribute fully. Lou has therefore offered us some pieces of advice around tension and conflict, and how to manage it effectively.

"The people around us shape how we see, experience, and interact with the world and ourselves. Relationships are vital for our development and survival; even today when we no longer have to worry about predators with large teeth trying to eat us. Our food, homes, sources of entertainment, and the nature of our jobs are all part of a process involving so many other people. However, relationships are also the greatest source of frustration, discomfort, and anger. The simple reason for this is because each of us are a complex muddle of all the things that make us, us," she says.

"So, my suggestion, quite frankly, is getting back to the real basics. Firstly, conflict comes from a point of view that threatens our own. We have spent our entire lifetime trying to make sense of the world. When someone tries to change or belittle that, it can be curious at best, cataclysmic at worst. The antidote is empathy. Empathy is not an acceptance of the other person's argument. It is not seeing from the other person's point of view. It is understanding why this person, with all the things that makes them who they are, thinks and feels the way they do in this moment. Using empathy, we can understand that they are a human too, someone who is also trying to muddle through life, just in their own way."

Secondly, Lou suggests asking yourself whether the source of conflict is their stuff or yours. Because of how we make sense of the world, we do not always realise that we are acting out an old scene rather than being in the here and now. This will come down to the relationship that we have with our feelings. Feelings are powerful because it is their job to help us identify what makes us feel safe and what makes us feel like we are in danger. However, they do not mature as quickly as we would like, especially if a particular feeling has been reinforced in numerous scenarios. This means that sometimes, when we are in conflict with someone, at least one of us is arguing with our past, instead of with the other person.

The antidote to this is to spot your patterns. Try to notice if there is a fight or a thought that keeps coming back and rearing its head at different points in your life. Does it come back to a recurring thought like 'I'm not good enough' or 'I do everything around here'. As unhelpful as it seems, this is your terrified anxious brain doing its best to protect you from harm. Acknowledging this is like calming a distressed toddler by giving them a cuddle and showing them that it's ok; or that it is not, and you can run away together.

"Stepping out of the old argument helps you address the issue and the person in front of you right now. It is liberating every party to handle what is in front of them, rather than this collective baggage," says Lou. "My third piece of advice is to be honest and ask yourself if it is really about right or wrong. This might put us on shaky ground so I will keep it relatable. I once asked, in a team social, 'Is peanut butter sweet or savoury?' and it blew up. It turns out that my team had strong divided opinions about peanut butter.

"Words like 'should', 'need', and 'has to' were bandied around as definitive truths. Here is an exercise for you: how often do you use these words in your day-to-day? Not just in conversation but also in your own inner monologue. The antidote to this is similar to point one. If someone describes or even hints that our actions or behaviours are wrong, bad, or incorrect, our anxious brain translates that as I am wrong, bad, or incorrect. Did anyone feel their protective barrier go up reading that?"

One way to navigate this comes all the way from ancient Greece. Socratic questioning is being able to debate an idea through asking questions out of genuine curiosity, free from judgement, a political agenda, and coercion. If we understand that someone believes in something based on their own experiences, then we might learn more about them and find a solution if we asked questions that would help us to understand them and their view. It might be their perspective captures an element that your worldview is missing and, by learning from one another, you could uncover a new solution or at least learn something new.

"Tip number four is to give yourself permission to disagree. Conflict is not always as easy as deciding which type of pasta goes best with Bolognese, or whether cream or jam goes first on a scone. When the stakes are higher, like a business or romantic relationship, it feels much harder. We go from collaboration to competition with people that we love, trust, and respect," says Lou.

"By believing that it is OK to disagree you bring several things into the situation. Firstly, it means you do not go into the space of trying to win, whatever that looks like. Secondly, it can help you empathise with the other party without having to take on their view, priorities, or agenda. Thirdly, it can help you decide what you want to do with this relationship after this interaction. If the outcome of the disagreement has a significant impact on the relationship it might be a helpful catalyst to look at the state of your relationship. As hard as it is to move on from an established relationship, if the disagreement indicates a fundamental ill fit, moving on can help both parties look for more productive partnerships in time."

The final piece of advice from Lou is to understand and use kindness. Kindness gets confused with so many other things, so let us start off with what it is not. It is not agreeableness, which is at best, passive and at worst, placating. It is not being nice, which is at best, supportive and at worst, conflict avoidance. It is not teaching or parenting, which is at best, enabling and at worst, a distrust of the person's knowledge or experience. Finally, it is not love, which is at best, loyalty and commitment, and at worst, duty bound by roles and expectations.

"Kindness is about giving someone the space they need to be who and how they need to be in that moment. That does not mean that it is ok for your line manager to shout at you for five minutes in front of your colleagues. To be kind in this scenario is to allow yourself to physically and emotionally distance yourself from the situation, to tell your manager that it would be better for you both to talk about this when they are calmer, and to find a space where you can process this experience in a way that is safe and natural to you. This space allows you to think more clearly about the situation and work out how best to move forward," says Lou.

"I get that this is overly simplified, and deliberately so because of the complexity of humans and their relationships. I write from my stance as a pragmatic optimist and the belief that everyone is doing the best they can with what they have. If you have a different opinion, I would, characteristically, love to hear your points of view."

Chapter Summary

My relationship history tells a story. From a broken engagement to an emotional affair, to finally allowing myself to love and be loved. Do not get me wrong, I have so much more to learn as my partner and I go on this journey together; about vulnerability and teamwork, and saying out loud some of the things that are going on in my head, but the lessons in this chapter are useful to bear in mind to grow as we go. Particularly that conflict is not something to be afraid of if it is handled properly.

The biggest lesson here is that those prior experiences need healing. They need acknowledging, accepting, and forgiving so that I do not make the same mistakes again. This will involve lifting the lid on some of the things that I perhaps would rather remain forgotten, so that I can make peace and find closure, whatever that looks like. Closure is not always possible in the traditional sense where one person apologises to the other, so it is important to find ways of drawing a line under it within yourself.

I wish I had the answer for how to do this, but it will be unique to you. What seems to work for me is finding something symbolic to hold on to. For example, I was once in a counselling session where I was asked what my biggest problem was. I told her it was the fact that I felt like I had a piece of me missing that was leaving a black hole in my chest. My counsellor asked me what I was going to do about it. The next day I ordered a necklace with a jigsaw puzzle piece charm on it, and everything changed. I had my missing piece, I was whole, I had no more reason to keep looking back.

And so I began the next chapter of my life. The beauty of the necklace was that when I wore it, whenever I felt that black hole starting to open up again, I could hold on to that charm and pick myself back up again. A couple of years later I changed that jigsaw puzzle piece for a compass, and more recently, for a charm engraved with my business' leaf logo. Each time I find a little more healing from the chapter of my life that has gone and a little more hope for the future to come.

In this chapter you have heard from...

Name: John Kenny
Name of company: John Kenny Coaching
Position in company / Job title: The Relationship Guy
Company website: www.johnkennycoaching.com
Facebook: @johnkennycoaching
Instagram: @johnkennycoaching
LinkedIn: https://www.linkedin.com/in/john-kenny-coaching
Twitter: @johnkennycoach

Name: Lou Chiu
Name of company: Lou Chiu Coaching and Consultancy Ltd.
Position in company / Job title: Culture and Relationships Coach and Consultant
Company website: louchiu.com
Facebook: @louchiucoach
Instagram: @lwychiu
Twitter: @lwychiu

CHAPTER SEVEN

Social Wellbeing

B en Thompson is the Director and Co-Owner of The Oxford Business Community Network, which was established in 2009 to offer networking based on the fact that people buy from people, not just the label that they represent. "We offer various networking opportunities to help you develop your business. From speed networking and online events to breakfast meetings, site tour events, socials, and round table discussions. This variety enables the members to continue their interaction, build an awareness of their expertise, and develop their relationships," he says.

"After being a member for four years representing my recruitment business, Thompson & Terry Recruitment, Founder of The Oxford Business Community Network Mike Foster invited me to partner with him to grow the business. It was a complete no brainer for me to go into partnership with my friend and well-respected entrepreneur, having been a networker in Oxfordshire for over ten years and been fortunate enough to lead a number of groups."

At The Oxford Business Community Network there are many large businesses on the member list, many of which invest in wellbeing and provide a strong support network to their teams. Equally there are several smaller businesses that are really strong and well-respected across the country but, just the nature of being small, normally means the owners need to wear many different hats. "It's worth remembering that most business owners started their career as an employee, with a strong support network around them which is certainly one of the benefits that gets forgotten during the excitement of becoming an entrepreneur," says Ben.

"In my experience, most business owners set up their own business because they are really good at their job, whether that is as a recruitment consultant or a decorator, but it is a very different skill to run a business. Of course, it is very easy and common for small businesses to outsource bookkeeping, marketing and sales, but much more difficult to outsource the development of wellbeing. There are most certainly experts that can help, we have a couple within our 100-plus members, but in my opinion, there is no substitute for the support of a community that many networking organisations provide."

The Covid-19 pandemic made it even more difficult for small business owners to gain the social interaction they needed, especially if that business owner lived alone or had to shield. Ben and Mike were incredibly conscious of this and made it their mission to provide that social interaction and network for their members. They believe their membership is about choice and so have offered a number of very different networking and social events over the last 12 years, including during Covid-19 times.

"It is so important to remember that some business people will want small intimate groups, others much larger events with 100-plus in the room. Some want really formal, and business-focused events, others more relaxed gatherings like a virtual quiz. We have learnt that, like with business, not one size fits all when it comes to supporting wellbeing, and we will continue to constantly find more ways to support our members in this way. Whilst it is often daunting to enter a new network, it is vital for any small business owner, especially during the formative stages," says Ben.

"In my experience of launching my own businesses and supporting many other businesses to do so, the adrenaline and excitement often prevents you from thinking about your own health. There will almost certainly be a bump in the road, whether that be after six days or six months; normally the point where you could do with more business, or a client lets you down. It feels so much worse when it is your business than it probably is in reality. A friend of mine, who was actually my manager towards the start of my career, always said when things go wrong in a small business they are never as bad as you think they are, and you probably will not remember it a year later."

Having someone who can say they have been there and done that is often the support many small business owners need; a soothing ear or advice from somebody who has actually got through it. Ben's experience has shown him that entrepreneurs want to help, and most will be incredibly generous with their time to ensure you avoid the mistakes they made. "I was fortunate that my networking journey had already started when I opened my first business, Thompson & Terry Recruitment, and I will forever be grateful to the close support network I had around me," he says.

"Once you start to attend events, my advice is to always be super positive and self-assured when talking to the room. Whilst most business people will want to help you, you are more likely to get customers if they feel they can trust you to do a good job with their money. The next step is to arrange one-to-one chats; it is so important to remember these should be a two-way conversation and be about you helping them as much as they helping you. If you keep following this process you will quickly find that you are starting to build a group of friends that will genuinely give you the support that you would get from working for a corporate."

When it comes to improving your social wellbeing, managing yourself is key. "Throughout my career I have definitely had spells where I have worked incredibly long hours and really put myself under pressure to do more work than feasibly possible, probably because there was not anyone above me telling me to go home and relax. My biggest advice is to really ensure you set boundaries, so you do not surpass a maximum number of hours and you are still able to spend quality time with your loved ones," says Ben.

"I think the most productive I have been in my career was when I took the time in the middle of the day to go for a run with my dog. This was so important to me as it gave me a chance to completely step away from technology and refresh. I think my final word is, remember to talk, people will want to help you if you ask. If you are having a bad time, tell your network. Throughout my networking journey there have been several people who have talked openly about mental health or financial issues. I know they were incredibly cautious to do so, but all felt so much better once they had, and were humbled by the level of support they received."

Supporting each other is also the message of Mindsight, wellbeing architects and cultural change consultants who, in May 2020, launched a unique, safe space to chat with a brew about the things that impact our everyday mental health. "Roast N Toast is fun, refreshing and non-commercialised; it is a space to share and benefit from thoughts, hints and tips. Roast N Toast is a place where you can come as you are. It is support for each other at all levels. Roast N Toast 1.0 runs every Wednesday morning from 9:30am and has impacted more than 300 businesses in its short lifespan. Its success has led to the need for more, so Roast N Toast 2.0, 3.0, and 4.0 are on their way," says Founder Dave Scholes.

As well as running Roast N Toast, Mindsight helps individuals, business, charities, and the education arena focus on their number one asset, themselves and their people. This is done in six ways. One, they increase awareness and understanding around mental health for all. Two, they remove the stigma and get under the skin of difficult topics and heartfelt matters. Three, they create space for honest, open conversations for all, in and beyond the nine to five. Four, they embed a positive culture of habits and behaviours. Five, they add a personal touch to support. Six, they provide tools and tips to make personal and collaborative decisions for self-care and for the care of others.

"Workplace wellbeing is not what we do. We are more than a tick box and workshop. We are a lifestyle change and a culture of support by the many not the few. We build well. Mindsight comes from the heart. A heart to do everything we can to help individuals to look after themselves and others in all areas of mental health and wellbeing. The power to make a positive cultural change is in everyone. Everyone has a story, and every story is powerful. Tell it in a way that only you can. Stories shape futures and save lives. It all starts with the 1% which is you," says Dave.

"Ten years ago, I lost my best friend to suicide and for many years I struggled to deal with it. I had a lot of 'what ifs' and questioning of previous conversations, things I had missed in meet ups, and responses I may have got wrong. This affected my own health. With time and a lot of help, I learnt more about mental health, how to manage my own situation, what expert advice is available, and what supporting others looks like. What I am good at is being me; a mate with an arm around and expertise in my own story."

Dave would describe Mindsight as having swagger. Swagger is not about arrogance, but it is about heart engagement and the confidence to ask for help or offer real support to others. Swagger is their care, their investment, and their game changer. They educate the head and engage the heart. "Over the past few years, I have had the privilege to be able to support people from all walks of life through crisis situations, prevention support, and more often than not, a helpful chat over a coffee or a beer," he says.

"From these experiences, from my heart, from the power of my story Mindsight was born. Flipping the focus on mental health, every one of our interactions will create at least six more positive engagements. The six connections model will impact thousands of lives. In May 2021 SIX CONNECTIONS launched as a very unique retail brand to help individuals support themselves and their friends. Real Conversations. Powered by Mates."

Also promoting group sessions is Jackie Robinson, Founder and Director of The Balance Approach. She is a qualified holistic therapist, and a qualified counsellor. "We offer wellbeing champions training courses, offered both online and in person. We also collaborate with wellbeing experts, and work with hard-to-reach communities, businesses, schools, and charities. Our aim is to increase confidence so that they too can become advocates for wellbeing, helping ourselves to help others for a happier, healthier life for all," she says.

"So, with this in mind, it was all about wellbeing and providing a wraparound service for corporate businesses and their employees, and to charities and schools. I did this by collaborating with a lot of people. I took employees or people from charities out of their workplace and delivered a full day wellbeing training day, which covered many topics around wellbeing. The wraparound service is looking at your financial health, looking at nutrition, doing things naturally, and not just relying on traditional or conventional medicine."

The Balance Approach promotes simple methods and the idea that everything we do is connected to our wellbeing. "I really promote group sessions to make it fun and not a chore or tick box exercise. The methods are all natural and do not discriminate, everything that we do focuses on prevention and we have even developed a course that can help prevent virus infection, and even serious diseases, by using herbs and vitamins. Our immune systems are amazing if we look after them," says Jackie.

"A friend of mine got breast cancer a few years ago and I just got into thinking about ways that she could help herself and looking for different alternative methods of treatment. I was already interested, but I got into it a little bit more. It did help my friend and she outlived her prognosis by five years and had a really nice life. Unfortunately, she did not survive but she made amazing memories for all of us. I was working as a social housing manager at the time, so I trained and qualified as a holistic therapist, and I also trained as a counsellor. I never set out to start this business; it has just evolved and will continue to evolve."

During the Covid-19 lockdown The Balance Approach had their third birthday and throughout the pandemic did a large contract for a charity that looks after the wellbeing of Black, Asian and minority ethnic (BAME) communities in Blackburn. "I absolutely loved it. I really did. I recognised as a holistic therapist that preventative health methods do not always reach some families and communities because it is not yet available on the NHS. It is essential we make a difference and by collectively working together this is more powerful and will narrow the disparities," says Jackie.

"I am very passionate about making a difference because we all can. So that is why I have set up another leg to my business, which is called the Balanced Community Approach CIC. Everyone is an individual and therefore should have a bespoke game plan to improve their health. Our programmes start with the why, what, when, and who; only then you can start with the goal setting; if you do not have a goal, how can you measure your improvements? My main piece of advice with this is that comparison is the thief of joy, so do not compare your journey with that of others as this is a sure way to fail your own personal goals."

Another part of Jackie's training that links into social wellbeing is around making memories. Jackie has courses within her training programme that are focused specifically on this. So often we do not think about making memories until after they are made, but we need to be intentional and plan these in to help with our wellbeing. The first tip that Jackie has around making memories are memory jars. "You can make your own with any kind of clutter, like glass jars, and you can actually paint them which is another way of making a memory; get your friends together or your family or the kids and paint the jars," she says.

"Every single day, you put in a memory in the jar and at the end of the month, you empty your jar of memories, and you look through them with the family or with friends. You might have thought a month has passed so quickly that you have not really done anything but as you look through, you realise what memories you have made. When you are actively thinking about making a memory or what memory you have done, you want to do more of it. I do not want a month where I have done nothing. So, you actually have to plan these memories in."

Other group activities, such as cooking, are good ways to improve social wellbeing. Jackie suggests thinking about the things that you like doing and how you could turn them into a social activity. "I love reading but then there can be months where I do not do any reading, because my mindset is too foggy, and I cannot think or concentrate. But, if you get a group of friends or family members together who like reading, or just get as many people involved as you can, over zoom or in person, you can take it quite seriously. This month, we are going to read this book, and we are going to discuss it, so it motivates you correctly," says Jackie.

"When you keep this in mind, you will be thinking about questions for the discussion and you are thinking more deeply about that book, instead of reading the book, and actually your mind is drifting off to other things. By being focused on what you are reading you are really thinking about what you are learning from it. This is the same for watching television. A lot of people have been watching more TV during the Covid-19 lockdown, which sounds like a bad thing, but is not always bad. There is a lot of good documentaries that can generate good discussion."

Jackie gives the example of the time when she and her son watched a documentary on mental health and because of what they saw her son then sent a text to every single one of his close friends, asking if they were okay. "We will always remember watching that documentary together and the impact that it had. So, memories are a lot of things; you are not always going out for a lovely meal and having a nice evening with family and friends. It can be a lot of different settings. It is about sitting down and thinking I am going to make a memory every single day. And you do not have to put pressure on yourself to do something absolutely spectacular; it is about spending time, quality time, in my opinion," she says.

Looking back is not always a positive thing, especially when there is trauma involved. Through her counselling, Jackie understands that you do have to be quite careful not to trigger bad memories. Therefore, Jackie's final tip on increasing social wellbeing is creating a vision board, helping people to look to the future. "I love doing these and I do them as often as I can, because my visions change. Every six months, I get more excited about the next project I have, not necessarily work, but a new aim. I've done these boards with groups before and it is amazing what comes out."

Jackie's collaborative approach to her work shows the importance of social wellbeing, not just for the individuals involved in leading or teaching but also for the participants. I am a massive believer in collaboration. I do not do it all, I am not a specialist in everything, and so I collaborate with a lot of different people. I think we need to hear different voices to raise the energies. It has also been really important to work together through the Covid-19 pandemic and hopefully we will come out of this better than we ever were before, no matter how difficult it has been," says Jackie.

Chapter summary

As an introvert I am usually pretty happy in my own company and can often stray into hermit territory. What has been interesting for me in this chapter is coming to understand that while I need time, space, and quiet to recharge, there are also wellbeing benefits to being a little more social. This is particularly true as a self-employed business owner, as it has been tough setting up during a pandemic, but it is good to know I am not the only one. Also, it benefits not only me but my business and the individuals who would benefit from accessing my services.

Outside of work, increasing my social wellbeing also has merits and rewards. I have an ever-increasing brood of nieces and nephews, and from what I have experienced so far, they grow up too fast. Creating and capturing memories of my time with them brings me so much joy, and looking back through photographs was a real grounding technique through our long separation during the Covid-19 pandemic. I love

Jackie's tips around making a conscious decision to create memories and it is something I would like to work on as life gets back to normal again.

My final point to make on social wellbeing is the broader impact that it can have. Nothing heals like bringing people together and for that we must learn how to accept differences, concentrate on similarities, and have open and honest conversations in calm and respectful ways. We can be the generation that puts to bed some of the longstanding inequalities that plague our communities, just as we are striving to be the generation that sees the end of the human race destroying the planet to our own ends. We are awake like never before and this presents us with limitless potential.

In this chapter you have heard from...

Name: Ben Thompson
Name of company: The Oxford Business Community Network- Business networking community
Position in company / Job title: Director and Co-owner
Company website: https://oxfordbusinesscommunitynetwork.co.uk/
Facebook: https://www.facebook.com/The-Oxford-Business-Community-Network-289417788393
LinkedIn: https://www.linkedin.com/company/oxford-business-network/
Twitter: @Ox_Biz_Network

Name: Dave Scholes
Name of company: Mindsight / Six Connections
Position in company / Job title: Founder
Company website: www.mindsight.org.uk www.sixconnections.co.uk
Facebook: @mindsightconnect / @SixCnnctns
Instagram: @mindsight_connect / @six_cnnctns
Twitter: @mndsght_cnnt / @six_cnnctns

Name: Jackie Robinson
Name of company: 'The Balance Approach' and 'Balanced Community Approach'
Position in company / Job title: Director and Founder
Company website: http://www.thebalanceapproach.com/
Facebook: @balance8 'The Balance Approach'

Instagram: @thebalanceapproach
LinkedIn: Jackie Robinson and The Balance Approach
Twitter: @BalancedCommunityApproach @BalancedCommun1

CHAPTER EIGHT

Recreational Wellbeing

“Having a recreational hobby or activity is so important to sustaining a high level of wellness. Just increasing your heart rate so you are breathing more heavily than normal will release the endorphins and dopamine hormones which will not only elevate your mood but help maintain a better cognitive function. That is right, you will be naturally nicer to other people. Studies have also proven that you are able to manage more complex tasks throughout the day and concentrate for longer,” says Owner and Director of SO FIT Group Ltd. and Swansea Outdoor Fitness, Phil Jones.

“Of course, most people know the additional physical benefits of sport and exercise, however, for me, it goes much deeper when it comes to your overall wellness. When we take part in sporting games, whether individual or team, you are setting goals, competing, and always trying to progress yourself as an individual. There is always something new to learn, a technique to master, this improves your personal development, and creates curiosity to question situations, which in turn will bleed over to your personal and professional life. This also stimulates intellectual, emotional and, if engaging in team activities, social wellness.”

Having spent just over ten years as a Royal Marines Commando, fitness and physical activity were a part of daily life and an essential requirement for operating at such an elite level. Whilst travelling the world and experiencing hostile environments such as deserts, jungles, and the arctic, Phil found that having a good physical state improved his mental state and helped him to be resilient. Whilst in the Marines, Phil played rugby, squash, and took up boxing. Recreational activity and keeping fit were also important for the long lengths of time on the ship where space was limited, and Phil consciously started to develop ways to keep active and keep his mind in good shape.

"To be honest, the transition from military to civilian life for me was not great. It took me a long while to really find myself. I realised that I wanted to help people, which I thought would be through joining the police or public services, but I really understood that affecting people's wellbeing and physical and mental health directly changed their life. That is what I then became passionate about. I did some further studies on mental health and the relationship between being physically active and working out with groups; that style of activity was a real game changer in the mental health world," says Phil.

"When you are in that group environment, that support network, you can rely on it, and you are not on that journey on your own. Whether it is a hill sprint or a couple more press ups, you have got people around you going through that same process. Leaning on that support network really helps to build your resilience. Afterwards, friendships are built and some of the longer-term members are close friends now, and when I see them helping each other get through the hardship, it is really, really important when it comes to mental resilience."

SO FIT Group was originally born from their sister company Swansea Outdoor Fitness, which started up as an outdoor fitness boot camp. As it progressed, it grew into more of a holistic approach to wellbeing, offering a lot of different alternatives to improving wellbeing, not just fitness. These included breathing techniques and nutrition, and that quickly grew into work commissioned by quite a big organisation. "We then went into the corporate side of things which is when SO FIT Group was born. SO FIT Group is the corporate element where we are health and wellbeing consultants for large clients," he says.

"Our aim is putting the fun back into fitness. We provide activities for children, but we also have members in their 60s and 70s. However, the activities we provide offer so much more than just fitness, they also encourage soft skills such as communication. I see it when people go into gyms, it is headphones on and head down; they do not converse anymore…

Confidence is a huge one too. I have got members which have come to me lacking in confidence and in social skills, and it has brought them on leaps and bounds. Another is basic motor skills, the hand eye coordination needed to catch and the mental working out of how a game should work or how they can achieve more in that particular situation."

When it comes to improving our recreational wellbeing, Phil has the following advice. "I often talk about re-engaging with hobbies that you might have had previously. That could be as simple as hillwalking or horse riding; it is still an activity, and it is still good for your wellbeing. Or you could try something completely new. Have a chat with your friends and see what they are doing and then go with them. Above all, pick something fun, step outside that comfort zone, and challenge yourself. If you can be around like-minded people, that is a bonus because that is going to be the key for longevity, and will also lift your mood and lift your emotional state," he says.

Combining work with veterans and children is a speciality of the Founder and Director of Allsports Coaches Coaching Academy CIC, Jim Prescott. "The idea originally started because I had taken early retirement from the corporate world and my youngest son had set up his own coaching business. I got involved when that started in 2008 and after ten years found we were still facing the same issues. Quality coaches are difficult to get hold of and difficult to keep since sports coaching is very much a gig economy sector. There is no formal way of registering coaches, so they can come out of college or university, and they do not have to register or keep up with Continuing Professional Development (CPD) other than a Disclosure and Barring Service (DBS) certificate and first aid," he says.

"One of the colleges that we were working in partnership with offered my son the opportunity to work for them full time and get a teaching qualification in the process, so I said I would keep my eye on the business and keep it going. His business partner also stepped away and so it came to me. This brings us to 2019 and I wanted to know what we could do differently, and who would make an ideal cohort that could come into coaching, maybe later in life, and decided that military veterans were that cohort. I spoke to peer groups who agreed and then came up with the idea to set up a CIC to train them, get them qualified and then get them into the community."

Jim also wanted to know what Allsports Coaches Coaching Academy could offer a school that was different from what was already out there. He realised that it was not enough to just offer sports coaching; if they trained the veteran as a coach to deliver mentoring for children with any mental health issues or general support needs as well, it would offer additional benefit not only to the children and the coach, but also to the school, the families, and the local community. Unfortunately, the Covid-19 pandemic struck before the initiative could get off the ground, but Jim is confident that once they are able to resume, the positive impact will be felt by everyone.

"At the beginning, our focus was on the social impact on children, on developing their life skills and support networks, but it will also have a big impact on the mental health of the veterans involved. As a result, we have now developed a series of metrics to use to monitor the effects and the value to the veterans and to the children as well as their families and the school themselves. For the veterans, we help to improve health and wellbeing, and employment or voluntary opportunities, which in turn impact on families. For the children, it is about educational attainment, teamwork skills, and encouraging children to talk," says Jim.

"As a direct result of the diversions over the last 15 months or so, we have developed a fully blended suite of training programmes that can be largely delivered digitally with face-to-face learning support as required. Delivery of our solutions will be supported by a fully integrated supply chain, and this includes Bright Star Boxing Academy who have recently been awarded The Queen's Award for Volunteering. Run by Joe Lockley and his team, they provide solutions for individuals via a range of programmes and have changed lives of many children and their families. We are delighted to have Joe on board delivering crucial elements of our training programme, as well as working together on several ventures that can make a difference to everybody involved."

Another veteran using their training and background to support recreational wellbeing is Sean Molino BCA. As a former British Army Physical Training Instructor who served within the 1st Battalion Welsh

Guards, Sean is now the Director of the Multi Award winning Forces Fitness Ltd. and Founder of the Veterans Awards CIC that operate in England, Scotland, and Wales. Sean was invited to the Palace of Westminster to be Awarded a British Citizen Award for his contribution to health.

"I joined the British Army in 1999 and chose to join the 1st Battalion Welsh Guards, with my 1st posting at Wellington Barracks in Central London. During my time in the Armed Forces, I completed a Junior Non-Commissioned Officer Cadre at Household Division and Parachute Regiment Centralized Courses gaining a Distinction, and also a Physical Training Instructors course at the Army's School of Physical Training, Aldershot. I served on many operations at home and abroad, and then transitioned from the Military into Health and Leisure Management before working as a Training Academy Manger for the largest grocer in Europe, before setting up Forces Fitness," he says.

"I firmly believe that positivity breeds positivity! My fantastic team and I have delivered health, wellbeing, and resilience building sessions to over 170 schools and 17,000 pupils so far. The sessions themselves are educational, providing the participants with healthy tips on fitness, wellbeing, and nutrition whilst working together in teams to overcome challenges both mental and physical. The main driving force behind these sessions is to try and slow the ever-growing obesity levels within children and young adults in Wales, and give them some healthy, easy to follow tips that will improve their overall health and wellbeing."

Each session is fun and cements the importance of working together as a team to solve the problems that are put before them, this in turn develops their social skills. "Feedback has been fantastic from all the schools and colleges that have participated in the challenge with a huge 98% of attendees wanting to take part in our activities again. In business it is not all about the profit but the investment we are putting into our future generations. Today's children are tomorrow's leaders," he says.

Over the years, Sean has appeared on multiple TV programmes all aimed at improving people's health and wellbeing. He was a part of the team for the TV programme Alfie's Angels with Gareth Thomas and James Thie on BBC1 Wales in series 1 in 2015, series 2 in 2016 and series 3 in 2017. Sean was asked to be an instructor on Alfie's bootcamps where he trained a group of ladies in preparation to take part in the Cardiff Half Marathon. He has also featured on BBC Radio 1 with Dev, and on the TV Programme "Let's get a good thing going" with Kevin Duala in 2018.

"Long before the recent Covid-19 pandemic, we all knew that physical activity boosted our health and ability to resist and overcome illness. That conclusion has not changed. In fact, it is more relevant now than ever. These are my top tips for taking care of your recreational health and wellbeing. Firstly, stay active. This does not necessarily mean beasting yourself in a Military Circuit. My advice is to try and stay active 3 times a week. This could take shape in any forms from walking, jogging, walking up and down your stairs, home circuit or yoga," says Sean.

"The important thing is that you are staying active and enjoying it. A great example that I can give you is if you like photography then get that camera out, get out for a walk and do what you love whilst staying active. Whatever your age or fitness level, there is an activity you can do. My second piece of advice is, embrace the outdoors; It is good for your mind and body. Recent trials have found that outdoor exercise is associated with an increase in energy and revitalisation as well as decreased confusion, anger, depression, and tension compared to when exercising indoors. It makes you feel better about yourself."

Research from the University of Essex confirms that when working out in the green environment it improves your self-esteem. Soak up the sunshine benefits. Get that well deserved Vitamin D3 from your outdoor sessions, it is important to your bone health and metabolic function.

Sean also suggests you keep learning. Continued learning through life enhances self-esteem and encourages social interaction and a more active life. "Every year, I try something new and keep learning both through accredited courses, CPD courses, or even just learning new training techniques or challenges that can help me," he says.

"Tip number four from me is to give back and support others. People who support and help others are more likely to rate themselves as happy. You can do this for people in many ways from giving advice to people, if you are qualified to do so, listening, having a chat if you see someone is down, or even supporting and helping financially like many Fundraisers do.

Next, I recommend taking breaks from technology. Social media and modern technology have taken over our lives. It can have a positive and also a negative effect, and we all need to take a break at times, whether it's not watching the news or taking a break from social media completely."

Recreational wellbeing can be highly social, but this comes with a note of caution from Sean. "Get rid of those people who constantly put you down and are always on your back, this goes for face to face and online. If there are people on your social media that only pop up to argue or constantly criticize you, get rid of them. They are not worth your time and not worth them influencing your mental health. Have a network of people who you can trust and who will champion you and support you when you need them."

Lastly, a healthy diet can protect the human body against certain types of diseases such as obesity, diabetes, and cardiovascular disease. "A good diet has a huge impact on our overall wellbeing and keeping us feeling fresh and in a good mood. My main top tips are to eat as natural as possible by consuming a high fibre, low GI carbohydrate diet, including sources of protein and good fats, plenty of fruit and vegetables, and a small amount of dairy. Try and drink 2-3 litres of water each day, cut down on your fizzy drinks, choose wholemeal over white, and aim to be good 80% of the time; we are all allowed a treat, do not let your diet run your life. There is no magic formula, however, I have certainly found that over the years the above have definitely helped me in my life journey. Keep smiling and do the things that make you happy."

Vicky Watson, yoga instructor, holistic therapist, and Owner of Infinite Harmony understands that when it comes to recreational wellbeing, sport is not for everyone. "Yoga is the closest you are going to get to sport with me. I think we all spend too much time in our heads, and yoga or other recreational activity allows me to get out of my head and quieten the noise in my brain. I also make jewellery and that is almost like a form of meditation while I am doing it as I am focused only on one thing. It allows me to detach and I think that is really important," she says.

"I started training as a holistic therapist eons ago. At the time, this is a long time before my children were born, I had been told that I could not have children and I was thinking about other things that I could do with my life. I had a traditional business career and I wanted to do something that was more spiritual, and more about therapy work. So, I trained as a holistic massage therapist and then as an aromatherapist. I suppose, because we had kind of given up thinking we could have children, I then fell pregnant, and so I could not do all of my aromatherapy because I couldn't touch the essential oils."

Fast forward 12 years and the job Vicky was working in moved to London and she did not want to go with it, and therefore, took redundancy. At the time Vicky had been doing yoga to help her connect with her body without feeling uncomfortable due to suffering from a condition called endometriosis which led to a hysterectomy. After doing a one-day yoga retreat, Vicky was blown away with the approach she saw and decided to use some of her redundancy to pay for the first year of yoga training.

Infinite Harmony was born at that point in 2016, and Vicky was able to pay her way through her second and third years of yoga training. While Vicky had not set out to be a yoga teacher, she has been able to grow the business ever since offering it alongside her holistic therapies, coaching, and since June 2021, Thai Yoga Massage. Vicky is also undertaking a postgraduate diploma in yoga therapy because she hopes to continue developing in the direction where the coaching and the yoga align.

"I do a lot of meditation work. I do Yoga Nidra, which is a form of yogic sleep and is incredibly relaxing. When you ask people, 'can you meditate?', you get 'oh, no, all I am going to do now is sit and think about what I need to cook for dinner or my shopping'. So instead of telling people to meditate, I offer Yoga Nidra sessions, which is a form of guided meditation, my kids call it a yoga bedtime story. People join via Zoom, often in their beds, in their pyjamas with the cameras all turned off, and I talk them into meditation, and they just go off to sleep. It is lovely," says Vicky.

"The Thai yoga is a therapeutic model. So rather than just doing a relaxation massage, you would focus on a specific area. If you had a problem with your neck, I would just massage that one part of your neck. We also talk about different layers of the body. You start with the skin layer, you then move into deeper layers of the body, using acupressure, acupuncture, and steam treatments, and I make a lot of potions. Aromatherapy in itself is a precursor to traditional medicine. And as long as you use it with respect, it can really help people."

When it comes to increasing recreational wellbeing, Vicky has found that one of the biggest problems is that we have lost connection with our bodies. Yoga then is helpful because a lot of the work involved is around that union between mind, body, and spirit. Vicky believes, that when it comes to pain or disease, we can sometimes blame or hate our bodies, but we must remember that every part of us is a part of the body. You may be experiencing this kind of disconnection if you find yourself being overly critical of who you are and what you look like.

"I think it is quite easy to just associate yourself with the things you hate about yourself, rather than the fact that your body is actually amazing. In particular, when you have had a long-term illness, it is very easy to focus on that rather than on your body doing amazing things to keep you going despite that illness. When you are talking to yourself, imagine you are talking to a small child. Would you say that to a small child? Why would you say that to yourself? It is about getting in contact with the child that is in you," she says.

"Yoga really does centre you back into your body and it gives you that space to relax. I think it is a more natural way of working with the body. But I would find and try as many different things as you can. So, if you end up going down the yoga route, for example, there are many different styles of yoga. I teach a variant of Iyengar yoga, which is a very precise form; it is a form of hatha yoga. There are also things like Ashtanga yoga, which is a little harder, and many others. I think when you are first starting out, see what is available, and try it."

Following this advice means you do not just get to experience different types of yoga but also different teaching styles. This is important because not everybody likes the way everybody teaches. "It is the same with coaching," says Vicky. "You would have a chemistry meeting at the beginning of a coaching relationship, to see if you click and I think it is the same with any form of therapy. If you look at yoga as a form of therapy, that is what I would recommend doing, however, you need to be open minded and give things a go."

However, Vicky explains that increasing your recreational wellbeing does not have to mean taking up any type of sport or class at all. "You could just go for a walk and look at the sky, and listen to the birds. Just take yourself out, that is a form of meditation. Look for those little opportunities and look for something good in the day. We have often done that with the kids; two stars in a wish. Ask yourself, what are the two stars for your day? And what is the wish? How would I do it differently tomorrow? I think we spend too much time focusing on the negative and we need to come away from that."

Chapter summary

Like music, sport is one of those things that has the ability to connect people of all ages, all abilities, and all walks of life. A few years ago, an ex-boyfriend of mine took me to my first football match at a big stadium and I could not get over the tribe mentality of the fans that were there to support their team. In their camp, at least, it appeared that everyone was equal, everyone was important, and everyone played their part in cheering on the side. I know it is not always like that, but it seems that whatever sport, hobby, or interest you have, there are always fellow enthusiasts for you to connect with.

If I am going to take my top three learning points from this chapter, as I have done for so many of the others, the first would have to be the physical benefits of sports and reactional activity. From the most adventurous workouts to the gentle relaxation of yoga, movement in all its forms is good for our bodies, whether the outcome is building muscle, increasing flexibility, or simply forcing us to get some natural sunlight and fresh air. Lockdown kept so many of us inside for so long, it is good to know that there are even just little things we can do to engage with the outdoors again.

Secondly, the mental and emotional wellbeing benefits of hobbies. From the hormones that are released to the skills that are learnt, to the community that is created, all of these help with our mental functioning and emotional happiness. It has been clear from this chapter that these are especially important for particular groups such as children, where the practice of co-ordination, strategic thinking, problem-solving, multi-tasking, and teamwork will serve them well as they grow and develop. Other vulnerable groups also greatly benefit from the opportunity to focus on tasks rather than allowing negative thoughts to spiral.

Thirdly, and finally, the power of sports, hobbies, interests, and crafts as a way of giving back. In 2017 in my role at the time, I was tasked with helping a group of individuals enter the Chester Marathon to raise money for a mental health charity for young people. I was amazed to see how many took part and that was just one sporting event on one day several years ago. Millions of people across the country take part in sponsored walks, runs, cycles, and dance-athons; charities accept knitted blankets and toys for babies and the elderly; schools hold bake sales; and in 2021, crocheted letterbox covers appeared as if by magic to brighten everyone's days.

It is incredible to think that so much can come from just a little bit of exercise. I know I had taken for granted the ability to go to the gym or to a class before the lockdown of the Covid-19 pandemic took that option away from me. I think this is a great time to reflect on why we used to get involved in these things and why we should again. How will you start to improve your recreational wellbeing? Go back to something you used to do or give something new a try?

In this chapter you have heard from...

Name: Phil Jones
Name of Company: SO FIT Group Ltd. and Swansea Outdoor Fitness
Position in company / job title: Owner and Director
Company website: www.sofitgroup.co.uk and www.swanseaoutdoorfitness.co.uk
Facebook: @SOFITfitnessandwellbeing
Instagram: @sofit_health_and_wellbeing
LinkedIn: https://www.linkedin.com/in/phil-jones-so-fit-group-ltd-25783344/

Name: Jim Prescott
Name of Company: Allsports Coaches Coaching Academy CIC
Position in company / job title: Founder and Director
Company website: https://allsportscoaching.co.uk/

Name: Sean Molino BCA
Name of company: Forces Fitness Ltd.
Position in company / Job title: Managing Director

Company website: https://www.forcesfitness.co.uk/
Facebook page: @forcesfitnessUK
LinkedIn: https://www.linkedin.com/company/forces-fitness-ltd
Twitter: @ForcesFitness
Instagram: @forcesfitness

Name: Vicky Watson
Company Name: Infinite Harmony
Position in company / Job title: Yoga Teacher, Wellbeing Coach, Holistic Therapist
Company website: https://infiniteharmony.co.uk/
Facebook page: @infiniteharmony.yoga
LinkedIn: https://www.linkedin.com/company/infinite-harmony
Twitter: @InfiniteHarmony
Instagram: @infiniteharmonyyoga

PART THREE

Connection to the World

CHAPTER NINE
Financial Wellbeing

" My business provides bookkeeping and administration services which I tailor to meet the needs of clients and businesses. My aim is to be more than just a bookkeeper as I believe there is much more to being a good bookkeeper than just doing the numbers," says Lara Bennington, Founder and Sole Owner of Blossom & Achieve. "I understand that every business is unique; that no two business owners are the same; and that while businesses may be in the same line of trade, they are all run in different ways and with different styles."

Lara knows that by being approachable her clients will feel able to contact her whenever they may need or want support, advice, or guidance. "I make the time to understand their business model, how they run things, what type of people my clients are, and how they work and learn best. This allows me to tailor the support I provide to best suit them and their business," she says. "I wanted to set up my own business that was more than just bookkeeping. A business where I help mentor and guide my clients, to help them develop and grow."

Most of Lara's secondary school education was focussed on sociology and psychology as her intended career path was to be in social work. However, a shortage of availability in social work courses meant that her university studies were redirected to business and finance. Lara was able to maintain the link to the sociology and psychology fields, as the business aspects of the course covered areas such as organisational behaviour and consumer marketing behaviours.

"Although I ended up with a career in finance rather than social work, I have never lost the desire to help and support others. After having been a bookkeeper as an employee for many years, I decided that I wanted to incorporate my desire to help others and my bookkeeping skills. In 2013 I set about making this happen. I wanted a business name that represented exactly what I aim to help others do. I used the B from bookkeeping and the A from administration to create my business name Blossom & Achieve," says Lara.

"My business is currently in its 9th year of trading. In that time, it has won a number of awards including the 'Small Business Sunday' award from retail entrepreneur and Dragon's Den star Theo Paphitis. My business has also gained a strong and solid reputation for being supportive and encouraging. Most of my work comes from client referral, and I have received a lot of glowing client testimonials. It is lovely to hear responses from my clients when they have contacted me wanting guidance on something they have not understood."

One of the most important tasks within a business is staying on top of your finances. "You might be a sole trader operating from your kitchen table or a limited company with office space and employees, but the finances are just as important whatever the size of your business. The financial data for your business needs to be not only organised and accurate, but also kept up to date so your data is always available in "real time". It can be a complex task as there are many different tax rules and deadlines, along with constant changes in rates and allowances."

Lara understands that financial data is a task that needs to be completed by someone with solid financial knowledge as financial mistakes can be both very costly and timely for a business to correct. "Many business owners find the subject of business finance stressful as they lack the knowledge and skills required. It is possible for your business finances to quickly get out of control, if you try and struggle with doing such an important business task not really knowing what you are doing. This creates pressures and stresses which reduce your ability to concentrate on the running of your business," she says.

"Having a good and reliable bookkeeper for your business can not only save your business finances from becoming a disastrous mess, it can also reduce those financial pressures and stresses. This then allows you to focus on managing your business and making the decisions your business needs with a clear head. You may feel nervous or exposed about having a bookkeeper, especially if you have existing financial problems when you approach them. It is important to remember, a bookkeeper is duty bound to treat all information you provide as strictly confidential, and a good bookkeeper will never be judgemental."

Lara suggests taking your time to make sure you find the right bookkeeper for both you and your business. If possible, find someone who has been personally recommended to you and look at reviews other clients have given them. You need to feel that you can completely trust them and always feel at ease to talk openly with them. Having a good rapport with your bookkeeper is particularly important. Even when you have a good bookkeeper and everything is up to date, organised, and accurate, there may be times when you are faced with problems out of your control, and quick thinking is required. Your bookkeeper should be someone who has a positive approach and is good at dealing with problems.

"Running a business of any size can be challenging enough. Finding a good bookkeeper not only gives you the reassurance that your financial records are organised, accurate and up to date, it can also positively contribute to your wellbeing. It can give you great peace of mind knowing you have access to someone whom you can talk to, who will listen, and provide support and advice. This in turn helps you to have both a successful business and that all important healthy work-life balance," she says.

Lara makes a specific point of regularly checking in on her clients to see how they are, and to make sure they are not suffering in silence. "Many people can feel too shy to ask for guidance, for fear of being considered weak. Reaching out and asking for help or an opinion, is in fact a huge strength and is certainly not a sign of weakness. At Blossom & Achieve there is no question, worry, or concern that is considered silly or daft."

On top of this Lara encourages her clients not to overdo things, not to take on too much all at once, to take regular breaks, and to find a healthy work and life pace that is right for them. She promotes positivity and open mindedness, working with clients to help them find the inner belief that they are capable, and how to be observant of and open to new opportunities. Lara encourages her clients to share their news and successes, and loves to see their excitement and watch them 'Blossom & Achieve'.

"Many people can find finance such a daunting subject and many are fearful of it. People can be fearful of finance whether they have financial worries or not. A lot of this fear comes from not having control of the situation. It is the fear that makes it seem as though the situation has control over you, hence the feelings of confusion and feeling out of your depth," says Lara. "The first step is to be 100% authentic to yourself. Many people who have financial worries can live in denial. If you are not honest about things to your inner self, you will never be able to change the situation or reach your goals."

Therefore, Lara recommends trying to keep your mind in the present whether you have financial issues or not. "People can dwell on what has happened in the past or get excitedly carried away on focussing on the future, but it is what you do in the present that determines your path ahead. Yes, it is good to have goals for the future. Yes, it is wise to remember past experiences and learn from them. But the key is to find a healthy balance so your focus is mainly on the present moment, as this is where you will make the steps to change the future," she says.

"Writing things down can be beneficial and again that applies whether you have financial worries or not. Having your budget or financial goals, for example to clear debt or to reach a savings target, written down can give you continued direction, focus, and motivation. If you do have financial worries, it can feel like a huge weight on your shoulders. Breaking the problem down into pieces and writing it out will immediately make it feel less daunting and more manageable."

Once you have done this, Lara suggests focusing on all the things you could do to improve the situation whether they be big things or small things. Then, take all your ideas and place them into three groups: short term, mid-term, and long term. "Many people think that solutions need to be huge and immediate. For example, if the problem was related to a credit card, they see just one solution which is to pay it off in full immediately," she says.

"The way that solution has been structured means it is not one they can make happen. They then think 'I can't solve this problem' and the problem remains, as does the stress, worry, and impact on their wellbeing. The key is to be openminded, break the problem down, and look at every possible option. With this example, the best solution might be a long-term solution, to set a realistic aim of say twelve months and then divide the remaining balance into twelve equal amounts. By doing this, although the problem is still there for the next twelve months, the important thing is, you now have control of it."

Having a manageable solution in place helps with your wellbeing as your worries will be eased. "However, if you feel like you are struggling, it is best to reach out for support. When people have financial problems, they may find it difficult or impossible to open up and talk to others about it, but trying to deal with such heavy issues on your own can drain you and impact your wellbeing in so many ways; poor eating habits, lack of sleep, withdrawing from interaction with others, and loss of concentration to name but a few. It can feel like a very long and lonely road."

"Look for someone with the traits of a good listener," says Lara. "A good listener will tend to ask open questions such as 'how are you?' rather than 'are you alright?'. Watch their actions over time to build up reassurance and the confidence to feel able to approach this person. Nothing is impossible, although, it may feel like it at times. Breaking the situation down makes it possible. It may feel like a long road ahead but each step you take, no matter how small, is a step nearer reaching the solution or goal. It is important to regularly make time to acknowledge to yourself the progress you are making; this will give you the strength and encouragement to continue."

It is important for us all to remain aware of not just our own situations but also of those around us. Individuals who are struggling financially need to remember the importance of reaching out to someone and actually talking about it out loud, and those who are not struggling need to be mindful that anyone can be suffering in silence, even those closest to us. This poem was written by Lara to be something that everyone can learn from and act as a reminder to us all.

Hiding behind a mask
On the surface I appear fine,
Underneath I feel lost.
I laugh and smile as we dine,
Inside I worry about the cost.

Do you see that I struggle?
That my outer image is just a pretence?
My finances are in such a muddle.
I feel I've lost all sense.

The truth is I feel a failure,
But I'm not brave enough to say,
I long for you to see and be my saviour,
As I really need help to find a way.

Can you see what I'm ashamed to admit?
What I don't have the courage to ask?
I really don't want to quit,
But I need help to remove this mask.

Another area of finance that people often struggle with is that of insurance. "We're trying to change the perception of insurance and all the negativity that can sometimes surround the protection insurance industry," says Sales Director and Protection Specialist of The InsureLife Group, Adam Kirkham. "We do this by taking away the stigma and jargon and speaking to people in plain English as well as providing, what we believe, is an unrivalled service and experience. For us, it is all about having a long-lasting relationship with our clients, and not something that is transactional and done with no care, thought or consideration."

This level of customer service was how Adam was first introduced to working in insurance. "I was approached by an existing client of mine who offered me a role within his general insurance brokers. He recognised that my skill set was easily transferable, and I had given him and all of my other clients a very high level of service over the years. So, I left my position as a manager of a local designer clothing store, for whom I had worked for nearly ten years, to work in the high-net-worth area of his team as a Business Development Manager," he says.

"This involved building on my existing relationships and introducing my client base to his very successful, well established, and multi award-winning business. I then progressed to working in the Financial Services part of the group and found my niche working within the protection arena. Having been diagnosed with cancer in 2016, it very much hammered home the importance of having good quality cover in place and the need for giving my clients the best service, advice, and products available on the market today."

This led Adam to start his own business in 2019 with his business partners John Stephenson and Dave Clapp. Together they formed The InsureLife Group and Forces Transition Group to allow them to help, give back, and add value to the civilian and military markets. Adam and the team deal with one insurer where their emphasis is on a shared values concept and is based around interacting with a plan where you are rewarded for being healthy. This means individuals not only get defaqto 5-star quality insurance but get some benefits and rewards along the way.

"We also see insurance as a way of giving our clients peace of mind that whatever life throws their way, they have the correct insurance in place and, most importantly, that it is going to pay out. Over the years that I have done this job and working with the military, I have found that often people do not have any plan regarding insurance. Perhaps they do not feel the need to have insurance due to having a great package with the military like a Death in Service or Free Income Protection if they are off sick, they get paid in full," says Adam.

"However, they can get to the end of their service and have no mortgage, no insurance, no will apart from their military one, no idea about their pension, and no knowledge of how to get any help on any of these issues despite, at numerous points in their career, having signed the '001' form. The 001 form covers the following six points:

1. I understand the benefits of my service pension.

2. I have considered the need for life and personal accident insurance.

3. I have adequate life insurance and personal accident, and if unsure, I should discuss it with an independent financial advisor.

4. I am aware of a list of financial advisors with particular expertise in service matters.

5. I am aware that comprehensive worldwide life insurance is available.

6. I understand the implications of not making a will."

This, along with the JSP100, which has in it a part about social mobility and taking ownership of these things, aligns to what Adam is trying to do for his clients. By helping them take control of these issues gives them a solid platform not just for their transition out of the military onto civilian street but throughout their careers. This starts with spending time with each individual to ensure that they and their families have the correct insurance in place moving forward.

For Personal Protection, The InsureLife Group offer Life, Critical or Serious Illness Cover, Income Protection, and Private Medical Insurance. Here, Adam gives us some of the top questions that we need to be thinking about for each one, starting with life cover. "Do you have a need and requirement for this? Do you have cover in place? If so, how much are you paying? How much cover do you have? What is the term? Is it fit for purpose? Does it just cover you or does it cover your partner or spouse? When was it last reviewed? When was the last time your advisor or broker spoke to you and checked in? Is your plan written into trust?" he says.

"In many cases the individual does not know the answers to these questions which is a problem. We can look at this to ensure they know and, more importantly, understand thereafter. We do annual reviews as well as checking in periodically throughout the year; this allows us to make sure that the client is protected as comprehensively as possible, as life changing events happen often, and insurance is not always at the top of peoples to do lists. We also strongly recommend that all our clients take the option of placing the plan into trust which gives a clear path of what is happening to the money by having a named beneficiary on there amongst other benefits this can offer."

For Critical or Serious Illness Cover the same questions apply as well as whether you know what conditions you are covered for; whether there are exclusions on your plan such as war exclusion; and whether your children are included on your plan? "Income Protection is next, and we find that a lot of clients do not know what type of insurance this is or how it works," says Adam. "It can be a lifeline, particularly on civilian street where people do not have sufficient savings to cover their bills should they be off sick and unable to work short to mid-term, never mind long-term. An income protection plan can cover a percentage of their wage providing they are unable to work and have a valid doctor's note, allowing much needed money into the household."

According to Adam, when it comes to Private Medical Cover there is a common assumption that it is expensive and unnecessary due to us having the NHS, which is superb. However, the strain felt by the NHS through the Covid-19 pandemic made Private Medical Cover a hot topic. "It is something that I chat to all of my clients abouts as it is important to give people a choice. We are here to advise and make a recommendation but ultimately it is down to the individual to decide what level of cover and what products they wish to proceed with," he says.

"I use the analogy that insurance is like sitting on a chair. The more legs you have on that chair, the less likely you will be to fall off. If you start taking the legs away, it becomes very much a balancing act. Most people will have some form of protection in place, the most common being life insurance as they want to have peace of mind that there will be something in place for the people they leave behind. However, you need a plan and a policy in place to cover as many bases as possible."

Adam and the team, work with clients to try and get them as many legs on the chair as their budget permits to give complete peace of mind, which is ultimately what people are buying. "I fully understand when I am with my clients that I am not talking about something sexy, and not always something they want. But, from my own ill health and having handled claims for my clients, I know it can take the stress away which links to our physical and mental wellbeing; can you put a price on that?" says Adam.

Also working in protection, but this time specialising in mortgages, is Serena Smith, Owner of Mortgages with Serena. "I assist first time buyers, remortgage / onward purchase clients, those wishing to do additional borrowing, debt consolidation, and of course, Life Assurance, Critical Illness Cover, and Income Protection," she says. Serena, like Adam, came from a customer service background. "I have worked in customer service based roles since I was 14; ensuring a smooth customer journey comes naturally to me."

Serena was tired of her industry being seen as a stuffy old condescending men's club. "I wanted to help other young independent women. I had a poor experience myself when purchasing my home and again when I looked to remortgage, there was no excuse for it. I am here to shake up my industry!" she says. "I have a very modern approach to my way of working, gone is the Monday to Friday, nine to five. I am here, and I am proud to offer a lot of free and helpful advice through my Instagram platform."

Also aware of how stressful it can be to get a mortgage, Serena feels that by being a process driven type of person her organised and efficient ways of working can help to relieve the stress of the process from the moment she is approached by a client. Serena is also a huge advocate of looking after yourself holistically, not just financial wellbeing but taking overall care of your body and your mind. Her 'previous life' as a personal trainer means that she has a very well-rounded approach to client care and believes that healthy minds start at home; it is not just about what you put in, and on, your body, it is about how you think and feel too.

But when it comes to getting a mortgage, Serena starts with the following advice. "You would not do the Christmas big shop without a shopping list and knowing you had the money to pay for it. So why would you make the largest purchase of your life without planning? First things first, find a mortgage adviser you like and can get on with, then find out what you can afford, you can then start looking whilst working closely with your mortgage adviser. This is not a quick journey. Be patient and trust that an independent whole of market adviser has your best interests at heart. We are usually self-employed, and our livelihood depends on doing a good job," she says.

"An adviser that works directly for a Bank or Building Society gets paid regardless and might only spend an hour with you before you are passed on to the next person in the bank's process; you get what you pay for in this industry. Seek advice from a whole of market adviser. Go with one you feel comfortable with as it is you that will be dealing with them, not your parents or other family and friends. Remember, the industry changes daily and you need a professional's help. Research is key. Look this person up, their reviews, social media, website, are they someone you would get on with?"

Chapter Summary

I once did some work with a youth charity, and we were discussing the topic of financial wellbeing. It was great to hear that as part of the work they were doing, the young people get taught about savings and budgets and general money management. I never had anything like this, but I think it would have been of benefit; not because I have found myself in too much financial difficulty, but just to feel a little bit less like I was scrabbling around in the dark when making big financial decisions.

So, what have we learnt from this chapter? Well, firstly, that money and finances can be complicated, especially as we move further and further away from having your pennies stuffed under your mattress and more towards only having digital transactions. Therefore, it is ok to need help and to seek that help form a specialist. Worry, struggle, and uncertainty only make things worse and can lead to mental, physical and emotional health issues.

Getting advice about a money problem is not a weakness, just as getting advice about a medical problem is not. Better yet is getting financial advice or knowledge before it becomes a problem, just as taking care of your body is better for you than waiting until you need a cure. Find someone who works in the industry and ask to have a chat, you might even want to consider taking a short course to build your knowledge.

Secondly, there are a lot of options for you to choose from in terms of people you can work with, so do your research and work with the person that works best with and for you. With anything personal like finances or mental health, relationships are key to success, so do not feel like you have to be or stay with a particular person or company because it is someone you know, someone who has been recommended, or someone you have seen before. Being able to get the support you need is the most important thing.

Thirdly and finally, remember you are not alone. Money and finances are a universal part of life in one way or another, whatever your circumstances are, there are other people who either are or have been in the same position. If you are struggling to reach out to a professional, then talk to someone you know and trust who might be able to help you in the short term or give you the confidence to take the next step.

In this chapter you have heard from...

Name: Lara Bennington
Name of company: Blossom & Achieve
Position in company / Job title: Founder & Sole Owner
Company website: www.blossomandachieve.co.uk
Instagram: @bandaservices
Twitter: @bandaservices

Name: Adam Kirkham
Name of company: The InsureLife Group- Insurance Broker (Protection Broker)
Position in company / Job title: Sales Director and Protection Specialist
Company website: www.insurelifegroup.co.uk

Name: Serena Smith
Name of company: Mortgages with Serena
Position in company / Job title: Owner
Company website: www.mortgageswithserena.co.uk
Facebook: @MortgageswithSerena
Instagram: @mortgageswithserena
LinkedIn: https://www.linkedin.com/in/serena-smith-82002b25/
Twitter: @serenarasmith

CHAPTER TEN

Occupational Wellbeing

"I was not overly academic at school and my people skills were not really valued, and mostly got me into trouble," says Director of DBKT Coaching, Kathryn Jeacock. "Expressing different viewpoints and asking questions about the purpose of what was being taught was determined to be insubordination rather than an opportunity to debate and discuss. At that time, I was not deemed 'university material' and it was not something that really appealed to me, so when it came to discussing careers, the only option presented to me was 'secretary'."

Kathryn left school uninspired and unsure about what the future held. "I only managed to stay a year at college before moving into full-time employment. Whilst my family and friends cautioned me against doing this, it was a key turning point in my life. This is because when I entered into the world of full-time work I began to fly; it turns out people skills are essential to getting on in business. I worked as a Receptionist at Oxfordshire Registration Services for Births, Deaths, and Marriages," she says.

"My line manager was a lady called Wendy, who saw something in me that not many did. She slowly nurtured my people skills and built my confidence to take on more and more responsibility. After a few years, I had started to take on more Human Resources tasks and Wendy encouraged me to study for my HR qualifications. I was really reluctant, following my previous experience of education, so Wendy invited a few people to come and speak to me about their careers."

One of those people was Nina, a HR manager who talked to Kathryn about the changes she had made to people's lives with her approach to HR and by supporting other managers. This resonated with Kathryn because the support and respect she had received from Wendy had helped her life start to change direction. So, tentatively and nervously, Kathryn started night school at college to study for her HR qualifications and found she loved every minute of it.

"I think it was because I could see the purpose of the learning and they encouraged discussion and debate, sharing of viewpoints and experiences. I immediately developed a thirst for learning about people and organisations. Over a number of years of hard work and having a baby in between, I obtained a first-class Master's in Human Resource Management. During this time, I recognised the need to gain greater work experience within the HR functions, so I left Oxfordshire Registration Service and joined another company working within the HR team," says Kathryn.

"I decided early on that I did not want to specialise or get pigeon-holed too soon, so I worked in a number of HR teams in different industry sectors, experiencing a wide range of HR issues and organisational challenges. For the last fifteen years I have worked my way up the corporate ladder and have worked in local government, food manufacturing, health and social care, logistics, automotive, and the technology and space sector."

Over this time, Kathryn has experienced the extremes of working life, from slow bureaucratic decision making, to cut-throat and aggressive commercial business; from the actions of employees impacting the lives of vulnerable people, to fast-paced and agile innovation. "Just when I think I have dealt with every people situation possible, another situation arises," says Kathryn. "What these experiences have taught me is that organisational change and people issues can be traumatic, and very often, organisational trauma is overlooked. Too often organisations apply policies and procedures that keep them compliant, but often overlook the humanity of the situation and the support that people need."

The more senior Kathryn became in organisations, the more she realised the lack of seeing the person behind the process and wanted to be able to help provide better support to people. "I also started to notice a movement in the style of people management and organisational development that is needed as technology continues to advance at pace. Then, the Covid-19 pandemic hit and overnight changes to the way many of us work accelerated. However, the pandemic did not just change the mechanics of how an organisation works, it also created a shift in how people feel about work," she says.

"Indeed, I was surprised at the impact the pandemic had on me. Despite the organisation I work for at the time, transitioning overnight to working from home and continuing to operate without the threat of job losses or furlough, the change coincided with a transition within me about what I was doing. My desire to do something more purposeful to support people was awakened by the Covid-19 crisis. The question was, what was I going to do? Could I really step off the corporate ladder I had sacrificed so much for and been so driven to pursue over the last fifteen years?"

Dealing with the change and transition within herself has been difficult, but Kathryn has seen it as an opportunity to learn more about who she is, and the impact change has on people. "I was lucky enough to be introduced to coaching early on within my career in HR and have adopted a coaching approach into my HR practice. However, it was when I qualified as an Action Learning Coach with the World Institute for Action Learning that I realised how under-invested teams are within organisations. Teams can be a great source of wellbeing or a source of dysfunction and conflict."

With the changes happening in the world and the need for organisations to change in order to operate within it, the reliance on teams to collaborate and work together is increasing. As Kathryn was working through what she wanted to do after her HR career, she started to see that coaching and working with teams was where she felt she could make the most difference to people's wellbeing within organisations; and so, DBKT Coaching was born.

"DBKT Coaching is a team performance coaching practise that seeks to elevate leaders and accelerate team performance in the changing world of work. We work with businesses to understand their challenges and co-create solutions that will deliver changes to ways of working that are sustainable, embedded, and future proof. Our solutions may include a combination of one-to-one coaching, team coaching, action learning, knowledge input, and HR support," says Kathryn.

"We help promote and develop wellbeing in three ways. The first is through dealing with change. We all find change difficult, and our one-to-one coaching can provide a safe space to work through the challenges and transitions that change creates within us. In addition, recognising that situations that happen within organisations can be traumatic for people, and providing space to support people and teams to work through that trauma enhances wellbeing and performance."

The second is through helping to build great teams. The people you work with can be a great source of motivation and inspiration, or a source of conflict, stress, and frustration. Working with teams to develop collaboration, ways of working, and building teamworking skills ensures a safe and fun space for diversity of thought, learning from failure, asking for help, and gaining support.

The third is in creating the 21st century organisation. Organisations need to change how they operate to create a culture of empowerment, allyship, autonomy, and collaboration, which supports the wellbeing of people in work.

Kathryn also has three top tips for improving occupational wellbeing. "The first is self-awareness. Being aware of the different parts of you, how you respond and react to situations, and how you are showing up to work is really important to understand, so you can be aware of your triggers and areas for development to support your wellbeing. The second is leaderships skills. We are all leaders in our own lives and as such we need to continue to build our leadership skills," she says.

"The leadership skills needed for the 21st century are changing. You do not need to know everything, and it is ok not to know. The skills you need to develop are around learning to team, problem solve, deal with change, have the ability to ask open questions, and know how to really listen to everything that is, and is not, being said. The third is learning mindset. You will make mistakes and you will experience failures; we all do, it is part of the journey."

According to Kathryn, the key is to make the most of these experiences and learn from them. This is why reflective practise is so important. Thinking about the experiences you have and reflecting on what went well and what could have been better will really help you learn and grow. So, too, will being open to learning from others, hearing different viewpoints, and being curious to understand through asking questions.

Justine Hodgkinson, CEO of Advocacy Focus, understands the importance of staff wellbeing in the workplace and has introduced initiatives to help improve wellbeing and culture. "When I began my role as CEO of Advocacy Focus, I soon realised that we needed to focus on culture, workforce development and engagement, and our marketing brand or shop window. I met a psychologist and approached him about working with me on the culture at Advocacy Focus and developed a strategy to ensure that the change process I was about to embark on was done with the team, not to them."

There then followed a significant and organic period of growth with a real focus on redetermining the organisational values, investing in the team, streamlining their services, and showcasing the impact of advocacy. Advocacy means supporting someone to become more involved in important decisions about their health and social care needs. One of the key developments for Advocacy Focus was investing significant time and resources into supporting staff mental health.

The Wellbeing Team at Advocacy Focus do everything from talking to the wider team about any ongoing challenges they may have, to delivering quarterly sessions such as mindfulness, and developing resources such as Becoming Your Healthy Self, which are free and available via the website. They also attend public events and community spaces, such as local colleges, to talk about mental health and tackling discrimination. They have even walked around town centres to encourage members of the public to open up about their own mental health struggles and wellbeing challenges.

"We signed up to a wellbeing pledge in 2015 and set to work on our action plan. It was a game changer for us. To this day we have an active Wellbeing Team, with wellbeing champions across all offices, and at the time of writing, have remained visible and accessible during the Covid-19 pandemic either virtually or at a safe social distance. We have implemented a whole host of things in the wellbeing space over time, to help our team turn up to work as the best version of themselves, which of course, benefits the people we work with in our communities. Some of the things we have introduced over the last five years are:

- Flexible working and dependency leave for employees with children or caring responsibilities.

- Employee Assistance Programme with a healthcare plan, telephone counselling and Doctorline.

- Face to face counselling services.

- All Fine Helpline, which is a daily duty manager being available for the team until early evening.

- Two thirds of our Senior Leadership Team are qualified Mental Health First Aid instructors.

- All of our team are trained in Mental Health First Aid, for both adults and young people, as part of their induction process.

- Birthday day off.

- Peer-nominated awards at our team meetings.

- Longstanding service award after five years.

- Annual leave increase after the three-year point.

- A weekly 'Active Focus' session with a qualified personal trainer via Microsoft Teams.

- Organised walks, socials, Christmas parties and bi-annual staff-away days.

- Annual participation in Mind's Workplace Wellbeing Index.

- Established a 'Female Focus' group in response to having a 90% female workforce.

- New or updated policies around mental health and wellbeing.

- Recognition of key members of the team to be champions in this area.

"Plus, a whole host of other things. We re-wrote our values as a team with input from our client group and stakeholders, and we embed them in everything we do," says Justine.

"We do not get complacent about our approach to this important subject and we are currently working hard to maintain our values-based culture during the Covid-19pandemic and as society recovers from it. As soon as the pandemic measures came into place, a key role of senior management was to motivate the team and ensure that they were all ok during an imposed period of isolation. We did that via motivational weekly emails, all staff webinars, and carrying out our quarterly team meetings via Microsoft Teams."

Advocacy Focus helps children, young people and adults who are facing difficulties or have difficult decisions to make. This can include how or where they are cared for, where they want to live, what their rights are within the process, or their ongoing care and support needs. Advocacy Focus provides free, high quality advocacy support that is completely independent of local authorities, the NHS, and Children and Adult Social Care.

"Our Advocates help people in the community who have difficulty or need additional support to communicate their thoughts, needs and wishes. Advocacy enables people to be active participants and central to the health and social care decision making process. Or, in the absence of a person's mental capacity to do so, Advocacy speaks up for that person when they are unable to do so themselves. Simply put, we help people to live the lives they want to live, and help them to achieve the health and social care outcomes that matter to them," says Justine.

"I had worked in the third sector for almost ten years when the CEO role came up at Advocacy Focus. My background had been in children, young people, and families, as a residential social worker, a regional development manager focusing on early literacy and strengthening families, and in a national role as Head of Early Years for a literary charity. Due to a change in personal circumstances, I applied for the role at Advocacy Focus as the job really appealed to me and their head office was conveniently in my hometown."

One of the biggest draws for Justine was that the role would enable her to contribute directly to her local communities and to see the impact first-hand. "The role is providing strategic direction and leadership for a charity that delivers preventative and statutory services for people accessing health and social care. I am responsible for our charity's effectiveness, strategic direction, funding sustainability, positioning our charity as the 'go to' advocacy provider, and demystifying and flying the flag for advocacy," she says.

This is a very personal role for Justine too as she had seen first-hand the impact on her mum when struggling to access services after a dementia diagnosis. Justine feels that advocacy is a little-known service unless you have been fortunate enough to have access to it when going through the health and social care process. Now Justine has a highly skilled and incredibly committed staff that eat, sleep, and breathe the organisational values and make a significant difference in our communities.

To help other managers and organisations support the occupational wellbeing of their staff, Justine has put together a few hints and tips that have come from her own experience. "Firstly, consult your team. Ask them what they want to see; carry out quick surveys to check the temperature in your organisation and ask your team what their key 'wants / would likes' are. You may be surprised by what they tell you but that is a great jumping off point," she says.

"Secondly, approach mental health and wellbeing as a strategy, and have a plan in place. Quick fixes or tick box activities may be good fun at the time, but they will not have a demonstrable impact. If you are short on time and resources, just do one thing well. Focus on a key aspect of mental health that will benefit your team or people. For example, stress, which is something we all experience from time to time, so it is an understandable and relatable first step on your wellbeing journey. The positive impact will grow from there."

Buy-in from senior leadership is essential. "Get people at all levels in your organisation to take your plan forward. Identify a budget for this activity, however small it may be. This will emphasise its importance and value. Once you see a return, and you will, you can invest further. The next step for us, for example, is to recruit a dedicated Wellbeing Lead. A positive, engaged team is the best advertisement for your business," says Justine.

"Next, keep an eye out on your organisation's productivity and bottom line. If you treat your people well and support them to be the best version of themselves, the productivity will improve, sometimes significantly. Ours did. That helps you make your case to further this type of work. Then, showcase what you do and the good news stories within your team. It shows the outside world that you invest in your people and that you are a value-driven organisation that would be good to work with and for."

Justine's next tip is to pool and share resources. "If you have policies that work, or ideas that help with engagement and wider wellbeing, share them. Working in silos does not help your team and it certainly does not help your beneficiaries or customers. Work together for the good of your team and the benefit of your wider community," she says. "Finally, never get complacent. Always strive to do better and to look after your team in a whole host of ways. It makes navigating through global pandemics a lot more straightforward."

But what if you work alone? How can you take care of your own occupational wellbeing? This is where people like Debbie Edwards come in. As Founder of The Omnipresent Assistant, Debbie offers remote executive and personal assistance to busy business owners, handling those non-income generating, time consuming tasks, which allows them to regain their most valuable commodity, their time. "I always champion the importance of looking after our wellbeing and place great belief in the power of positivity," she says.

"I promote wellbeing practises to the clients I work with, giving them tips and guidance that they can adopt and implement to ensure they are working in a healthy manner and can manage their stress levels. Along with this, I also produce blog pieces regarding issues within health, both physical and mental, which are published on my website, my LinkedIn page, my Facebook business and personal pages, and my Pinterest account."

Much of Debbie's career has been in employment supporting business founders and directors as an executive assistant. This was a great role for Debbie as it played to her strengths of being process driven, detail orientated and self-motivated, and she found she naturally excelled in this capacity. The last five years of working in these roles saw her working remotely, which she very much enjoyed as it opened a world of flexibility for her which, as a mother, was a game changer.

"As a result, I decided to make the transition into the world of self-employment, offering the services in which I excel; those which I have honed over the years, those I enjoy the most, and those which I know I can deliver exceptional results on. I was also keen to manage my own schedule after going through an unpleasant divorce which had the potential to interfere with my working life if not managed," says Debbie.

"I did not want to risk my mental wellbeing suffering more than necessary going through a difficult time in my personal life by putting myself under undue stress at work. As a result, I now run a successful virtual assistant business, where I am supporting business owners to help them regain control of their time and grow their business, whilst reinforcing the importance of mental wellbeing, reducing stress levels, and providing the support they need whilst being the confidante they want."

The core services offered by Debbie include project management, campaign launch support, event planning and management, SOP and policy creation, and documentation and social media management, along with general administrative support. Debbie also promotes safe ways of working, for example, ways in which you can sit correctly at your desk to ensure you do not cause bodily harm from straining. As such, Debbie has agreed to share her six top tips.

"Working within an administrative capacity often means spending long periods of time sat at a desk, looking at a Visual Display Unit (VDU) and usually not having taken the time to consider workstation ergonomics. This takes its toll on our focus and motivation, and can have negative physical influences on our bodies such as putting strain on our eyes and affecting our mental health," says Debbie.

"Sitting for long periods of time can affect our life expectancy. Couple that with our increasingly sedentary lives as a result of technological advances that help us in the home, and we are on a short path to several lifetime issues such as cardiovascular problems, carpel tunnel, neck and shoulder strain, musculoskeletal strains, heart disease, cancer, the list goes on. There are, however, practices we can implement to make sure that we look after our physical and mental wellbeing with minimum disruption to our roles, ensuring we work in a safe and healthy environment."

The first piece of advice from Debbie is to take regular breaks. Use an alarm if necessary, to remind you to stand, stretch, and walk around for two minutes regularly throughout your workday. Stretch your arms, roll your shoulders, twist at the waist, and give your body a good stretch. This will help combat muscle fatigue. You should also change your posture every ten minutes and take a full stand-up break twice an hour to ensure a healthier working day.

"The second is to look at your workstation set up. Be sure to use a desk, do not sit with your laptop on your lap. Objects of heat on our lap can cause skin problems and other issues. Ensure your desk space is set out so the things you need are comfortably within reach without the need to stretch. Check the height of your monitor is aligned with your line of sight. If using a laptop, make sure you do not need to look down when using it as this causes neck pain with prolonged use. Invest in a foot and/ or a back rest. Your knees should be at a 90-degree angle when sat," says Debbie.

"The third is to be more physically active. Our lives are more sedentary than our great-grandparent's. Cars now mean we do not walk as much, and housework is not the manual labour it used to be. As a result, we do not move as much in the modern world unless we find ways to introduce more physical activity into our day. Ideally, you want to have two and a half hours of activity each week. Choose to take the stairs instead of the lift, park a little further away from the door at the supermarket, etc."

The next tip from Debbie is snack control. It is easy to fall into the habit of mindless eating with desk-based work. This can be a fast-track to heart disease. Be mindful of what you are putting into your body. This includes the amount of caffeine too. Be sure to take full lunchbreaks away from your desk, be present when you eat, and drink water regularly. Mindful eating is healthier for you and will make you feel better from the inside out.

"My fifth tip is to visit the opticians. Did you know that the blue light emitted from your devices is harmful to your vision? Eye strain can affect our vision and cause headaches. Make sure you give your eyes a rest from staring at that screen. Manage your workload so that you naturally get time away from computer. Make sure you have regular checkups too, our eyes are so valuable," she says. "Finally get some vitamin D. Not getting enough sunlight can make it harder for us to get a full or restful sleep.

Lack of sunlight can affect our concentration levels and wellbeing, even more reason to get outside."

Chapter summary

I love being self-employed. This is partly because my last corporate role did not end so well with what started as a mishandled breakdown in communication resulting in disciplinary action being taken against me. It was a painful, lonely, triggering and stressful experience, which I would not wish on anyone. However, what came from it was a beautiful realisation that I was meant to be somewhere else, doing something that brought me joy.

However, one of the biggest struggles for me and my occupational wellbeing is loneliness and feeling isolated, especially through the Covid-19 pandemic. This is where occupational wellbeing links with social wellbeing and the need to network, engage, partner, and chat with other business owners or people in my field. One of the benefits of this book and bringing all these people together is that we have become a little Connected family and I am incredibly grateful for that.

Debbie has been working from home a lot longer than me or anyone who had it forced upon them during the Covid-19 lockdown. Her advice has been useful, particularly around blue light which might help with my migraines. I also need to be more disciplined about where I work. I have a great desk set up, but I often find myself working from the sofa. However comfy it may feel at the time, I know it is not good for me long term.

In this chapter you have heard from...

Name: Kathryn Jeacock
Name of company: DBKT Coaching
Position in company / Job title: Director
Company website: www.dbktcoaching.com
Instagram: @dbktcoaching.com

Name: Justine Hodgkinson
Name of company: Advocacy Focus

Position in company / Job title: CEO
Company website: www.advocacyfocus.org.uk
Facebook: @AdvocacyFocus
Instagram: @advocacyfocus
Twitter: @AdvocacyFocus

Name: Debbie Edwards
Name of company: The Omnipresent Assistant
Position in company / Job title: Founder and Virtual Assistant
Company website: www.theomnipresentassistant.com
Facebook: @Theomnipresentassistant

CHAPTER ELEVEN

Environmental Wellbeing

Maddy Lawson is the Founder of Rising Wild, a private coaching practice specialising in nature-led personal development for women. She is also Co-founder of Folk + Field, a social and educational platform that brings people together to learn more about living and working in alignment with the rhythms and cycles of nature. "My work is based on the belief that the natural world is not something 'other' or 'out there', but a holistic ecosystem to which we belong. Humans are part of nature. Humans are nature; composed of, and reliant on, the same fundamental elements as all other living creatures," she says.

And yet the prevailing social narrative asserts that we are somehow different. Separate. Superior. Where once we were in partnership with the earth, we have come to dominate and exploit her. Where once we moved with the rhythms of the seasons, we have come to fight against them. We have built walls that divide us from the land, referring with distance and detachment to the world beyond our windows as 'the environment' rather than our wild home. In addition to this, we have created artificial sources of heat and light, we buy plastic-wrapped products from supermarkets, and we clothe ourselves in synthetic fabrics, and allow their microfibers to pollute the soil and sea.

"I once heard the primatologist Jane Goodall say in an interview that we share 98.6% of our DNA with chimpanzees, and what has set us apart from them in our evolution is our development of intellect. She explained that she was always careful to call it intellect, a fairly clinical term, rather than intelligence which has connotations of emotional awareness, because although humans have evolved superior skills in many areas, we are also the only species to have ever contributed so significantly to the destruction of our own habitat. Surely, this can only have happened because we no longer recognise ourselves as natural beings," says Maddy.

"The narrowing of perspective from an ecocentric to an egocentric way of life is doing great harm; not only on a planetary level but on a personal one. Our sense of self has become so over-emphasised and so focused on individual human importance that we no longer think collectively or systematically. We no longer see ourselves in relationship with nature, meaning, we have lost our awareness of the ways in which our minds and bodies are affected by the ebb and flow of natural cycles. In moving away from a life guided by the agricultural year to a society governed by industry and technology, the presiding metaphor for human existence has become that of the machine."

Unlike the natural world, which honours change and rest, and imperfection, the world of the machine demands consistency and continual progress. But humans are not machines, and striving to meet that relentless expectation to function at our highest level of productivity all year round only leaves us feeling depleted, disheartened, and disconnected. Just as an apple tree lies dormant in winter, blossoms in spring, and fruits in autumn, we humans are cyclical beings too.

"We feel called to retreat within during the colder, darker months; not just physically, in terms of spending more time at home, but mentally too, tending naturally towards greater inward reflection," says Maddy. "In spring, it is common to feel a tentative stirring of energy and motivation as the snowdrops begin to emerge in February, which swells into a stronger desire to embrace plans, projects, and socialisation once the cherry trees are in bloom and the fields return to green. On a smaller scale, some people find that their sleep patterns are affected by the lunar monthly cycle, and others, such as those who struggle with Seasonal Affective Disorder, are deeply impacted by the cycle of the sun."

Maddy believes that approaching personal development from a nature-led perspective invites us to come home into our wildness; to reconnect with the lost part of ourselves that holds an innate natural knowing. It allows us to acknowledge the ways in which we are influenced by cyclical and seasonal rhythms, and to try and adapt our thinking and behaviour to allow more space in our lives and work for necessary changes of pace or direction. Embracing our wild self also encourages us to look to natural processes for guidance when navigating periods of challenge or change, and to cultivate respect for all living things, which in turn, reminds us to do the same for ourselves.

Now, through individual and group coaching programmes, workshops, and immersive retreats, Maddy supports women at all life stages to explore and expand their sense of self by cultivating a deeper relationship with the natural world. Her work with Folk + Field is similar but takes a broader approach, exploring human-nature connection through courses, seasonal gatherings, and an online membership community. "I started a blog and an Instagram account in 2017 to create an initial platform for conversation, and just over a year later I hosted my first nature connection retreat," she says.

"The response was so positive that I knew there was potential to develop the work into something deeper. I completed an introductory coaching certificate in 2019, having also set up Folk + Field with a good friend the same year, and I am now working towards a Postgraduate Diploma specialising in nature-led development coaching. My childhood adventures with my parents instilled in me a deep love for the wild world that has stayed with me into adulthood, and continues to uplift and inspire me every day. Our family holidays nearly always had nature at their heart, and you would find us staying in bird observatories on remote Scottish islands or pegging down a tent along the Cornish Coast."

This ongoing relationship with nature has helped Maddy through some difficult times, most notably when she began experiencing anxiety and depression whilst studying for a master's degree in 2010, and ultimately caused her to withdraw from the course. Maddy says she was very hard on herself about that decision but daily walks in the park or the countryside offered her welcomed moments of contentment and calm, a feeling of unconditional acceptance and an escape from the critical voice in her head.

"I had always been someone who planned every aspect of my life with meticulous precision and, until that point, I'd had a very clear plan for my future. After withdrawing from the master's, I began to realise that the life

I had been working towards was not really the one I wanted; I had reached the edge of my carefully drawn map to success and did not know how to move forward without its reassuring guidance. This uncertainty and lack of structure fuelled my anxiety further," says Maddy.

"I tried out a variety of career options over the next couple of years, but none of them stuck. I felt lost and unsteady, lacking the necessary conditions to put down roots and grow. Throughout this time, I continued to spend more and more time outside, and found that observing the details of the changing seasons offered me a new kind of structure, a reassuring reminder that life is cyclical rather than linear, that fallow periods are a necessary part of the process, and that winter is always followed by spring."

Maddy began to explore the concept of nature connection in more depth, drawing inspiration from a wide range of sources including contemporary scientific research and ancient earth-centred spiritual practices. "Through translating my findings into my own day-to-day life in ways that felt helpful and meaningful to me, I began to consider that there must be other people out there struggling with challenges or changes who would find the same sense of comfort and guidance through nature," she says. Therefore, Maddy has put together some tips to help people get started.

"The first thing I would encourage you to do is spend time outside daily, even if just for ten minutes. It may sound basic and obvious, but it is essential. It is often assumed that nature connection is a complex process that requires a lot of time or access to an awe-inspiring location, and that is not the case. It goes without saying that spending a week alone in a forest or up a mountain would make it significantly easier to tune yourself into the wild, but with conscious effort and practise it is possible to create space for connecting with a sense of your own wildness in your local park, in your garden, or even on your doorstep."

The very act of spending intentional time outside every day, whatever the weather, is an important step in its own right. We have been conditioned to seek engagement with the natural world only on our own terms and describing warm sunny weather as 'nice' or 'good' and cold or rainy days as 'miserable' and 'bad'. By letting go of that judgement and choosing to treat the outside world with unconditional acceptance, we begin to create a relationship of equality rather than control.

"Beyond embracing all weathers, seek to engage your senses in as many ways possible. Really pay attention to the small details of the things you can see, touch different textures or stand barefoot on a natural surface such as grass or earth, listen to the sounds around you, and notice any scents in the air. Taste is a little harder to explore unless you are a confident forager, but even taking a cup of seasonal herbal tea outside and noticing its flavours can be a simple way to engage with taste," says Maddy.

"On a longer-term scale, you could try keeping a nature table or nature journal to collect any seasonal treasures you might find or record the details of the changes you notice as the weeks and months go by. This can help you to feel grounded in the present, and to build an awareness of how each phase of the yearly cycle looks so you can connect with it more deeply when it comes around again. Similarly, making an effort to learn more about the things you see in nature such as birds, animals, trees, and flowers, can help you feel more at home in natural spaces."

With so much more she could suggest, Maddy leaves us with the following. "To get started on that inner work, begin with shifting the framework of your thinking from ego to eco by relating your experience to natural metaphors, embracing flux and flow rather than constant productivity, and acknowledge your role as part of an interconnected ecosystem rather than an isolated individual. You might also like to try tracking the effects of nature's cycles, whether that is seasonal, lunar, solar or menstrual, on your energy levels and emotions to help expand your awareness of the ways in which you change throughout the day, month or year."

As well as retreats like those offered by Maddy, there are other ways that you can connect with people as well as getting out in nature. Matt Gibbs is the Managing Director and Lead Instructor for Walx Preston, a community of people who love exploring the great outdoors, meeting new friends and building their health, fitness and life experiences while having fun. "We provide walks under our dedicated formats of Explorer Walx, Total Body Walx, Wellness Walx, and Community Walx," he says. "We have a rolling schedule of weekly Walx across Preston, South Ribble, and Chorley areas."

The Walx Preston objective for the 2020 decade is to reach 10,000 people in the wider Preston area and beyond, to encourage, motivate, inspire, and support them on their journey to better health, life experiences, and friendships. You can find out more on their webpage or through their informative social media content. However, to fully experience what they are about, you can join the group on their Drop-In Walx or online socials. So how did it all come about?

"In 2010, I went for a cholesterol check up at the GP surgery after my mum encouraged me, or verbally twisted my arm, to go for one. My parents, both approaching sixty at the time, had recently been for an age-related health check and had elevated parameters. Without having previously realised it, I suddenly found out the truth that I was three-stone overweight, had elevated blood pressure, and had bad cholesterol readings. I did not appreciate the gravity of the situation at the time, but I had unwittingly slipped into a lifestyle that was out of alignment with my true self," says Matt.

"In fact, taking a wider view of myself, I had chronic back and neck problems, I was unfit, I had a lot of bad habits with eating and drinking, and I was unhappy in my job. The straw that broke the camel's back, or rather the trigger point for me to start on a journey of lasting change, was the day I could not lift my then four-year-old son onto his bunkbed. At 35, and feeling like I was 50, I knew that he would only get older, taller, heavier, stronger and faster, and if I wanted to be the role model father to him then something had to change. Starting with me."

Matt knew intuitively that if he did not do something with his own health, fitness, image, feelings, and thoughts, then he would slip further into an abyss where he would likely lose all motivation to get out of it. "In these very moments, I was becoming increasingly aware that my actions truly influenced and affected my experiences, my relationships, and my success in life. Through trying to understand and overcome the many challenges I have faced with my health, my finances, my relationships. beliefs, habits, etc. I began to delve deeper into the research and the science, attend professional training courses, and explore how to effect lasting positive change and growth in myself and others."

In the end, Matt found that it was all quite simple and clear. Nobody really likes change. Also, to become the vastly improved version of yourself takes years of consistent, daily action of downregulating the things that are not good for us whilst upregulating the things that are. As a result of this, we learn that every step forward can be a challenge and that is the reason we require the help of two things: we need to lower, breakdown, or remove the obstacles or barriers in front of us; we also need helping hands around us to push, pull, guide, support, or cajole us forward and over these obstacles and challenges.

"The vehicle I chose to support other people to achieve these changes is walking. Why? Largely because walking is already something that we can do, but for the majority not often enough and not in a way that provides us with the multitude of benefits I have learnt we can get out of it. I tend to say that we co-create the environment for people to feel safe in stretching their comfort zones in a non-judgemental and supportive way. I encourage people to get onto our walking conveyor belt. It does not matter where you are with your health, emotions, connection with others, skills and abilities, financial status, background, or life experience. There is always room for growth and improvement," says Matt.

"However, when you move into a space where there is a collective of other people who are positive and also eager to make gradual, incremental, but permanent changes to their health, fitness, and life, then you acquire a framework to hold on to during the challenging times as well as confidence in knowing that someone will have your back if and when you are faltering. The inevitability of life means that no matter how positive, healthy, skilled, or focused we are, we are never too far from risk, pain, challenge, or problem. Yet, as we build our physical, mental, social, emotional, and spiritual muscles, we become more steadfastly resilient to whatever tough times we may come across in the future."

Being in nature provides us with a magical elixir of benefits. The sights, sounds, and smells of nature positively reintroduce us to our own human need for connection with Mother Earth and with others. "Sadly, in the modern world all the clothing, concrete, glass, technology, and artificial light that surrounds us in our office-based environments has disconnected us from that, yet we often struggle to see the correlation," says Matt.

"Exposure to nature not only makes you feel better emotionally, but it also contributes to your physical wellbeing, reducing blood pressure, heart rate, muscle tension, and the production of stress hormones. It may even reduce mortality. One of the strongest psychological benefits related to having an enduring relationship with nature is increased levels of happiness. Getting out walking in nature, particularly with others, offers a significant boost to your physical health, mental wellbeing, and social interaction."

While our immediate and local environments can contribute to positive wellbeing, so can exploring places a little further afield. Strawberry Holidays Founding Director Kate Holroyd knows this all too well. "Travel is an important aspect to your wellbeing. Generally, people understand the significance a holiday can have, but they often do not make a direct link between travel and wellbeing. As a traveller you escape the routine, the activities, and environments that you associate with stress. The escape from these situations, even just temporarily, is a huge release of negative emotions," she says.

"I find that travel helps me to reinvent myself. It expands your mind if you let it. From learning valuable lessons, to experiencing other cultures. Different is no better or no worse, it is just different, and seeing this permits you to re-evaluate what is important and what you value in your everyday life. I think experimental travel is especially good at this. It also boosts your satisfaction and happiness. On holiday you have a legitimate excuse for that extra glass of wine or pizza at breakfast. Indulge without guilt."

Kate has worked in the travel industry since she left University. "To be involved in such an inclusive, diverse, and exciting industry is fantastic, and I am grateful for every day. I got to the end of my tether in a marketing role that I could not get behind. I kept an open mind when looking for new roles and was approached by Global Travel Group to become a travel agent. The meeting changed my life and I have not looked back. Owning my own business has given me the challenge of my life, but I would not change it for the world," she says.

"When I am the creator of your next holiday, your load of responsibilities and travel planning pressure is lightened. With an extensive knowledge and expertise on tours and cruises for the USA, Australia, Greece and Disney destinations, I go to my exclusive network of providers, do the research, and collect quotes on your behalf. I will then present to you the most imaginative and memorable itineraries that reach beyond your journey and destination, direct to your inbox on a personal webpage with a link you can share and view on any device. You'll enjoy a dedicated concierge service; just think of me like your holiday personal assistant, with you every step."

For some people, the thought of planning a holiday brings them out in hives. Therefore, Kate suggests using an expert, such as herself, as they will create a holiday or a trip in a fraction of the time it would take you to do it yourself and at no extra cost to you. An expert will also look at your objectives for the trip and any concerns you have, and accommodate them into their recommendations. For example, if you want privacy and seclusion, they may recommend a private villa, or if you want to kick start a wellbeing journey, they can help you look at a wellness retreat.

"Another tip for improving your environmental wellbeing through a holiday is to get inspired. Even if you cannot get away right now, carve out time in your week to plan a trip. You could use it as an incentive or reward, or just a way to escape. There are tons of YouTube videos that show 360-degree views that you can immerse yourself in. Also, get creative. Some of the best destinations can be overlooked because they are a little harder to get to since they are not a well-known tourist spot, but they are often the best reasons to go," says Kate.

"Take yourself out of your comfort zone, it will help you grow. I would never feel confident in a bikini at home, but put me on a beach full of strangers and I strut the water's edge like a catwalk. Your inhibitions are lowered on a holiday. Even planning a trip can boost happiness and, of course, it is never as scary as it is in your head. Holidays are also great places for rest, plenty of sleep, good food, and great company. You will have amazing experiences and have plenty to talk about at your next dinner party or get together."

A specialist travel agent finding wellbeing in a change of environment is Alex Brooke. "I am the owner of Alex Brooke - Not Just Travel and currently developing my own brand Needful Travel, to specifically focus on health and wellbeing journeys. The aim of this is to help people collect memories instead of things, and to embrace the idea that all travel should enhance our wellbeing through whichever source and activities we individually feel will meet that aim," she says.

"For one person that might be a solo yoga retreat in St Lucia, for another it may be climbing with friends to Everest Base Camp, for families it might mean an activity-based holiday, or for corporate groups this could be a golfing trip or cruise that caters for plenty of social time and exploration when not in business meetings. For me, that may be a rollercoaster trip with my husband across the USA with some true escapism from daily life. It was during my BSc Honours degree in Business Operation and Control at Salford University that I earned a place on a one-year exchange programme to Toledo University in Ohio where my love for travel and rollercoasters beyond Europe started to develop."

Alex and her husband were married in a helicopter over Walt Disney World in Orlando in 2000 and have since done several road trips to ride the best rollercoasters in the USA. During that time, Alex was working in the energy sector, which she did for twenty years, and always meticulously planned her time off to enable fun packed and enriching holidays for the two of them. However, Alex had always wanted to work for herself and despite a very successful career, felt like she did not belong where she was.

"I decided to pursue my dream after realising that my skills in project management, business management, people skills, and my developed hobby of travel planning all fit well with the requirements of running a travel business. Not Just Travel presented the perfect way for me to achieve this through The Travel Franchise and I have not looked back since launching in 2017. I provide travel related services including discovery, planning, booking, and post-booking support for adventure seekers looking for new experiences," says Alex.

"I am primarily focused on active, experiential, wellness, group, touring, eco, cultural, and expedition travel. However, all types of travel, break, holiday, anniversary, celebration, sporting event, or excursion can be catered for through our arrangements as part of Hays Independent Group with access to over 350 suppliers and 2000 tour operators. Having an excursion or trip planned that you know will maintain or enhance your wellbeing and life experience is one excellent way of providing your mind with a positive focus, especially during particularly busy or difficult times."

That being said, Alex also suggests considering your wellbeing as part of your daily routine as well as planning longer periods of time out to concentrate on this important aspect of your existence. "Mindfulness and meditation are great tools plus strengthening, stretching, and stamina building exercises. It is also highly beneficial to gain ongoing advice from local coaching experts in the wellbeing field, who can help you to ensure you are placing enough emphasis on wellbeing and keep you on track if life events are taking over and affecting your overall health."

Chapter summary

I love the advice in this chapter. I love that we are starting to wake up to the fact that we are a part of nature and that our connection with the world around us starts within. I did not grow up with a garden, but my parents always actively encouraged us to spend time outdoors and I remember doing a lot of camping as a child. I am incredibly proud of my mum who delivers outdoor activities in the grounds of the primary school she works at, and I wish those kinds of initiatives had been available when I was younger.

I am now blessed to live in a very green area where it is common for me to see from my window deer, rabbits, frogs, birds of prey, and livestock, but I'm having to learn a lot with regard to keeping my plants alive. During the lockdowns of 2020, I spent a lot of time walking and it had many benefits for both my physical and mental health. If you do not want to walk alone or do not know where to start, then a walking group such as Matt's is the perfect solution.

Also, I can never recommend enough the power of travel. I spent three and a half years of my early twenties living and working in New Zealand. To date, I have been back twice since then and it never fails to fill me with awe and wonder, and inspiration. If you can have a spiritual homeland, New Zealand is mine and I look forward to the day when I can visit again. I have also been on humanitarian trips and girl's holidays, and UK-based weekend breaks, and each time I feel renewed and refreshed. If you can get away, anywhere, I would always encourage you to go.

In this chapter you have heard from...

Name: Maddy Lawson
Name of company: Rising Wild and Folk + Field
Position in company / Job title: Founder (Rising Wild) and Co-Founder (Folk + Field)
Company website: www.risingwild.co.uk www.folkandfield.com

Facebook: @risingwildcoaching / @folkandfield
Instagram: @rising_wild_coaching / @folk_and_field
LinkedIn: Maddy Lawson

Name: Matt Gibbs
Name of company: Walx Preston
Position in company / Job title: MD, Lead Instructor
Company website: www.walxpreston.co.uk
Facebook: @walxpreston
Twitter: @walxpreston

Name: Kate Holroyd
Name of company: Strawberry Holidays
Position in company / Job title: Founding Director
Company website: https://www.strawberryholidays.co.uk
Facebook: @strawberryholidays
Instagram: @kate_strawberryholidays
Twitter: @holsstrawberry

Name: Alex Brooke
Name of company: Needful Travel Limited trading as Alex Brooke – Not Just Travel
Position in company / Job title: Owner / Director
Company website: alexbrooke.notjusttravel.com
Facebook: @alexbrooke.NotJustTravel
Instagram: @alexbrookeneedfultravel
Twitter: @AlexBrookeNJT

PART FOUR

Connection to Purpose

CHAPTER TWELVE

Spiritual Wellbeing

❝ It is often the little things that can make the biggest difference: a new bud on a plant, a flock of geese flying overhead, a smile from a stranger on the other side of the road, even the reflection in a puddle. Of course, we need to be willing to notice these often small and easily missed moments to feel inspired. Noticing involves awareness and self-awareness. Having a balance of focusing inwards, within yourself, and outwards, outside yourself will offer great benefit. We can consciously place our focus outside ourselves in order to notice those things that can inspire us in our lives," says Helen Reuben, Owner of Purple Tree Training and Coaching.

"We coach people from all backgrounds to set goals for wellbeing. We also develop and train groups and teams to deliver skills and strategies for wellness and emotional health. We offer coaching in resilience and wellbeing, performance, and careers. Our workshops for staff include change, , leadership, motivation, and confidence, working relationships, and team events. We also have accredited coaching skills training programmes to advanced level."

Helen understands that when we have problems or feel low, we may find ourselves focusing inwardly on our emotional difficulties and challenges. Therefore, consciously focusing outside ourselves can be a helpful way of refocusing the mind from problems connected with past issues and situations to a way of being present in the here and now. "Being present is one of the best ways to enhance emotional wellbeing. When you are present, your mind is not trapped in the past or obsessed with the 'what ifs' of the future," she says.

"Triggers for inspiration are all around us, for example, visiting a place you enjoy being in. Having a simple change of environment will offer new stimuli for the mind. If you are unable to go there, then allow yourself to visualise and notice in detail this place of beauty or relaxation. Your imagination is a great ally and, when there is positive focus, it can enhance wellbeing. What do you see? Think about the shapes, colours, textures and forms. What do you feel? Are you calm and relaxed or uplifted and energised? What do you hear in this place? You can also imagine smells and tastes in this place of inspiration. The more details you are willing to notice, the more present you will be."

Sometimes there might be blockers to fully engage in activities like this. If you find you are struggling, it might be useful to ask yourself the following questions: what unwanted thoughts or feelings are you holding on to? It might be useful to acknowledge that you get to choose what you focus on, what you say to yourself, and how you feel. Every moment presents a new opportunity to let things go. "Also be aware of what you are saying to yourself. Aim to be kind and compassionate as you become aware of your inner dialogue. You may consider affirming a positive thought about yourself, for example 'I am willing to be open to new ideas and inspirations' or simply 'I am enough'," says Helen.

"The imagination has proven highly beneficial in many approaches aimed at emotional and mental healing. Also, in the world of sport, the athlete or sportsperson visualises success. For example, the footballer imagines taking a penalty and kicking the ball into the back of the net. See it as you want it to be and repeat this exercise two or three times a day, with the more detail the better. Not everyone finds it easy to see an image in their mind, yet we can imagine feelings, sounds, tastes, and smells that are linked to a positive outcome for you."

Your imagination is powerful, and one approach is to access one of four elements to visualise letting go of certain emotions or thoughts. Helen calls this a symbolic technique. Wind can blow away negative thoughts; you can use this element to visualise seeing and feeling the negative thoughts leave; water such as ocean, lakes, or rivers can wash away heavy negative feelings and emotions; using this element you can visualise the water washing away the unwanted thoughts and feelings leaving you feel cleansed and fresh; fire can burn them away; and earth can be used to visualise burying them deep in the ground.

Helen recommends keeping a joy journal to support and improve transcendental wellbeing. "A daily entry into a joy journal can help; as you note down these wonderful things you notice that they uplift and inspire you. You may even want to cut out pictures, images, texts, words from magazines or papers that give you a positive feeling or make you smile. Examples include: a beautiful sunset or sunrise, a quote from someone you admire, a postcard from a place you have visited or would love to visit, a cartoon that made you smile, something that reminds you of a happy childhood memory or a photograph of a happy time," she says.

"Remember to be kind and compassionate to yourself, forgive those who have hurt you and forgive yourself as well. Learn to be present more often; with your mind focused on now, you will avoid worrying. Develop and practise simple techniques to release unwanted beliefs, habits, and thoughts. Believe that you can change your habits and develop more helpful patterns of thoughts and emotions as well as empowering beliefs about who you are and the world around you."

One of the places you perhaps would not associate with spiritual wellbeing or mindfulness is the Armed Forces, however our next contributors are showing that presence of mind is key in all aspects of life. Major Pat Burgess, MBE of the British Army, delivers mindfulness awareness session briefs across Defence called 'Mindfulness - Plain and Simple'. "The talk shows service personnel how accessible mindfulness is, and challenges a lot of the misperceptions of the approach. I also created an eight-week online course for Defence and that has also been broadcasted on external channels through the Army Media Cell," he says.

"In addition, I have designed and delivered an eight-week mindfulness course, which I had endorsed at my own cost, by The Counselling and Psychotherapy Central Awarding Body (CPCAB). This was initially available locally, but now that the Covid-19 pandemic has shown new ways of working, it is available using Zoom. I am currently hosting a weekly mindfulness session for Defence that has an audience of between 14 and 40. I also released some short YouTube clips and practices for anyone to access during the pandemic. I am introducing mindfulness into Physical Training too."

After a highly kinetic operational tour of Afghanistan in 2009, Pat noticed that once soldiers returned having struggled with their experiences overseas, the support offered was not relevant to what they needed. Pat decided to do a degree in Psychology with a view to becoming a counsellor. Whilst undertaking the degree he happened upon mindfulness, and having already done some reading around it, he knew this was the path he had to embark upon.

"Not to be critical of other approaches to help, I felt that they were too microscopic in their dealing with human suffering and that mindfulness provided the holistic approach that I had been searching for. An accessible, disciplined, and simple practice, with the West Coast stigma removed, provides the perfect way to keep soldiers holistically fit. Recognising this was not my primary role, I offered my services to introduce personnel to mindfulness, this led to an obvious identification of need which I am trying to address," says Pat.

"The Ministry of Defence (MOD) formed the Defence Mindfulness Steering Group (DMSG) which is chaired by a three-star General, Lt Gen Rob Magowan. This group and my own understanding of chain of command gave me the artistic license to exploit any spare time to teach mindfulness in the organisation. Initially, the idea was to tie the approach into the Army's mental resilience and awareness programme. However, due to their increased workload and lack of staffing, mindfulness fell by the wayside. The courses, talks, and approaches that were created are Defence-wide, including Civil Servants and Contractors. I have also conducted some external training for schools, charities, and prisons."

Pat's longest running project has been to incorporate mindfulness into physical training. Physical Attention Training has had one pilot course, with a second to follow in due course. If the gathered data proves the course to be effective, then the approach will be offered to Physical Training Instructors across all three services: British Army, Royal Navy, and Royal Air Force. "The Military recognises the benefits of a mindful approach, but also recognises that it is a benefit that cannot be learnt overnight. A great deal of investment is required to truly realise the benefits, and that can be challenging to achieve in such a large and fluid organisation," he says.

"Mindfulness is 10% intellectual and 90% experiential, so my advice would be practice, practice, practice. Become familiar with the approach, maybe create a new routine by going on an eight-week course and then experience the benefits of disciplined and authentic application of mindfulness. Once you know it, from the tips of your toes to the top of your head, you will feel compelled to pass your knowledge to others. You can increase your depth of understanding an experience by attending a retreat, however, there are some unscrupulous providers of one-week, zero-to-hero mindfulness teacher courses that I would avoid."

The beauty of mindfulness is that it allows you to recognise that you are the key to your own wellbeing, the responsibility lies with no one else. This is an important message as John Stephenson, Business Development Director at Forces Transition Group well knows. "A service leaver will sleepwalk through the last 12 months of service, in most cases, and restrict their streamlined success, usually creating a less than adequate job role. This has a negative effect on those leaving and their families, and can create a mental health issue," he says.

"My advice would be to plan early. The later the plan the harder it is to succeed and the more the negative issues occur. The only person that can change your life is you, ownership from the very beginning of transition is key and the beginning of moving forward. The longer the sleepwalk, the harder it is to wake up. Use family and friends to see you through, but always remember you are the future, and you are the person that will make it work. Be positive and remove the negative out of your life, negative areas will drag you down."

John completed 22 years exemplary service followed by a poor transition into the civilian world. Now John is able to offer CV writing services, professional network set up, CPD confirmation, insurance and pension expertise, personal performance advice, job opportunities, and pre-interview techniques through Forces Transition Group (FTG). "The FTG have developed a programme named 'The Evolution of the Service Leaver', the aim is to extend this into the serving person and increase their thoughts of the future by changing the culture," he says.

"The evolution must start with an understanding of who you are. This allows the individual to document what they do, what their skills equate to and how to move forward. A CV is written next, giving a clearer direction and focus of the future, something the service person has never done before in their life. Add to this a network of contacts and a reason to grow it, allowing the service leaver to gain confidence and begin enhancing their elevator pitch, something missing in forces leavers. Apply similar thinking to the areas of social mobility, pensions, investments, mortgages, finance, and insurance, and the individual can be sure they will arrive in a new world alongside their family in a safe place physically, mentally, and emotionally."

To finish, Forces Transition Group provide job opportunity and hopefully the job instead of just a job, which a service person will generally move quickly from. "Stability is key for the first few years after service. Working alongside outside agencies helping with stress and anxiety also gives each person and their family a chance to realise that what they feel is normal. Always remember, no matter what, that everyone feels this way. Do not copy or think that everyone is doing better, as they are not. Be you, be humble, and be amazing," says John.

"The pack herd mentality of the military family is now different, and you must believe in yourself. Go your own way, be sure to take advice, but be sure it is what you want and not what people expect you to be. Stop chasing the title. Getting these areas right, everything else will fall into place and the wellbeing of the individual and their family should be a positive one without too much negativity, allowing for a smooth transition."

Knowing and being yourself is cornerstone of the work of Robyn Harris of Equenergy: W·I·L·D Wellbeing. "The term Equenergy comes from a combination of equilibrium and energy. I believe that when we get our energies back into balance, we experience wellbeing in a very natural way. I am passionate about bringing in nature, of 're-wilding' ourselves away from all the conditioning that we just absorb as we grow up. We adopt the rituals and routines of our families, we are influenced by all the things that our relatives teach us, and we apply their way of living in our own lives, and then we go out into the world, and we pick up all the culture and all the conditioning from the different places that we go," she says.

"But that is not necessarily who we really are deep down. So, for me, it is about looking at Mother Nature as an inspiration and guide as to how to get back to the nature within us. When we are not ourselves, we feel like a square peg in a round hole. We are not comfortable in our own skin, and we start to think that the messages that are out there are the right thing, and we are somehow wrong. We stop trusting our own intuition, and we are always looking outside for the answer. And there are ideas out there, but when we are trying to live up to them, we are never going to hit the mark; we are always going to feel that we are missing something. That is when the whole inner critic and imposter syndrome comes in."

Robyn believes that if we could just go within, become still, listen, and trust our bodies, then we would find that the answers, and the resources we need are inside us. "This has been my own journey. I was in a place where I just felt so low, and was at the point where I wondered if it was ever going to change. I was looking out there for all the answers; I went to the doctor, I went to counselling, but nothing was giving me what I wanted. I wanted something that felt sustainable, felt uplifting, felt nourishing and nurturing. For me, the pills were not going to do it, talking therapies were not going to do it, so I did a lot of reading and research."

A lot of what Robyn found to be helpful was around consciousness and awareness, and the whole idea of being the change you want to see. "Only you can change the things that need to change. It must come from within. But once you change on the inside, then everything changes. When the way you look at something changes, the thing itself changes. When you start changing how you think, and your perception, and your perspective, you change the whole chemistry of your body. The idea of sharing that with people is my passion, because I saw how much of a difference it made in me, and how those 'tiny little things' make a huge difference," says Robyn.

"I have four pillars now that I work to and share with people, and they spell out the word WILD. The W is for Wonder, I for Intuition, L for Love and loving yourself, and D for Dance and dancing with life. I love nature and I love the fact that life is messy. We live in the wilds of Wales, and we are surrounded by nature. It is not possible to fully manage it or tame it. A lot of it just does its own thing, but what it does is something amazing. It is the same for us. If you plant something and it does not thrive, you change the environment in which it lives, you do not change it. So, if my environment is not benefiting me, I ask myself, what can I change? That can be outer or inner environment: my thoughts, my beliefs, my diet, my exercise, the people I hang out with, what I read, what I watch, what I listen to, everything."

In line with the theme of the book, Robyn says she very much believes in the interconnectedness and interdependence of everything. "When we are thinking about wellbeing, it needs to include the mind, body, and soul; it needs to be the emotions, the physical, the cognitive, the social, the spiritual; it needs to be our whole environment, the inner and the outer. So just bring all of those elements in and look at the balance of them all, and think about how you can spend more time with the different aspects and bring more of them into your life. It is about approaching everything with openness and curiosity, without labelling and judging, and just asking: what learning can I get from this? What growth can I get from this? What information can I get from this? Then we can increase our overall levels of wellbeing," she says.

Robyn's main focus is on one-to-one coaching and mentoring; however, she also offers Emotional Freedom Technique (EFT), also known as tapping. "As a starting point, I get clients to write a timeline, and then I do an analysis of that, because I do a thing called MetaConsciousness, which can be very, very specific in uncovering the root causes of a disease, which can be targeted directly. For example, when exploring the root cause of back pain, I might discover the person's posture is contributing to their discomfort. However, when looking deeper I can see that their posture is due to a sense of poor self-worth.

Once the self-worth has been addressed and improved, the posture may automatically sort itself out, enabling the individual to stand tall, be proud of who they are and hold their head high which will go a long way to relieving their back pain. I offer a three-tiered Transformational Journey programme. The first step is doing the analysis and starting work on what we find. The next level is going deeper on that, and then the final level is more supporting the person as they start to spread their own wings," she says.

On top of this, Robyn offers workshops as well as having an open Facebook group and a closed private group for her paid membership subscribers. All the work that Robyn does has an underlying message about energy and the belief that everything is vibration. "If my head brain, heart brain and gut brain - so my thoughts, my words, my actions, and my beliefs - are in the same vibration, then I'll be in a state of flow. If not, then my energies are scattered, and I do not feel grounded or centred, I am not working with myself; I am working against myself, and it is exhausting. So, bringing these into alignment and congruence just feels so much more uplifting, empowering, energising, exciting, and fun," she says.

"Understanding that was a big shift for me in my journey because I had lost my sense of humour and my husband kept telling me that I'd had a sense of humour bypass. I could not laugh, and I did not think I had anything to laugh about! Now, I spend my whole time laughing - laughing with myself at things. With my workshops I do not give a set programme to follow. It is more about saying to people, these are the tools, take the tools and adapt them for your situation, and for yourself as an individual in your situation. I prefer that to saying: here is an instruction, which is the same for everybody, off you go."

In order to check your alignment and get in touch with yourself, Robyn regularly encourages people to do a body scan, to tune in from the top of their head and then go down through their body, asking how each part is feeling without labelling it as a good or bad feeling. Recognising what we are feeling allows us to build a vocabulary to recognise when we are in a flow and when we are not. This gives us an awareness of what state we are in, and then we can start to work out how to get from A to B. It also helps us to recognise what triggers us into feeling a certain way, and what we might need to do more of, or to remove from our lives.

"For those that want to engage more with mindfulness, I would suggest asking yourself what you do where you just lose all sense of time, feel 'in the moment' and in the zone? It might be looking at a sunset, it might be singing, it might be playing an instrument, it might be going out for a run or being out in nature. Then, ask yourself how you can get to that feeling more often and build up from there. Start off with just gentle exercises of mindfulness, maybe sitting for two minutes, or one minute, or 30 seconds, and just notice, because that is all it is, just notice and observe," says Robyn.

"Sometimes, when people think spiritual, they think church, or religion, or they think 'woo woo'. But for me, spiritual is anything that helps you to be still, to go within, to connect with who you really are, to connect with the fact that who you really are is so much more than what we can see, and to connect with the knowledge that we are all linked. I am interconnected with the environment in which I live and with the world around me, and I am connected with every other being on this planet, whether that is a person, an animal, or a tree. If you watch the sunset, and you can get into that 'wow' of the sunset, that to me is spiritual."

Chapter summary

I must admit I was a little nervous when it came to the title of this chapter. I knew what it meant but I was conscious that it might put people off. However, I think the contributors that are involved in this topic really do justice to the practical, albeit intangible, aspects of spiritual wellbeing as well as tying it in to the overall themes of connection and holistic wellness. Just as we are a part of nature, we are also soul and spirit, and the more we can engage with some of these, perhaps lesser-known, aspects of wellbeing, the healthier we will become.

From this chapter I have learnt that it is up to you to take charge of your wellbeing whether that is your diet, your career, or your presence of mind, nobody else can do it for you. Yes, as this book has shown, there are many people that can help you, but ultimately, it is down to you to understand who you are, what you need, and how to fill any gaps. It seems obvious, but only you live inside your body and your head so only you can tell if something is different or off. This requires self-awareness.

The second thing I have learnt is to have that awareness without judgement, and to be kind to yourself. Mindfulness and meditation are skills and they require practise so try to not be hard on yourself if you do not connect with it instantly or you do not feel like you are doing it right straight away. Patience is kindness and one that, if you are anything like me, is much easier to show to others than to ourselves. I am laughing at myself as I type this because of the number of times I have almost given up writing this book, because it has not gone perfectly to the plan I had in my head.

The third, is to look for the little things. As the saying goes "not every day is good but there is good in every day". For me, increasing my spiritual wellbeing means taking the time to stop and breathe, and look for some of these little wonderous moments rather than waiting for something big to come along. My garden has been an amazing help with this as I am able to watch how the seasons change the flowers, the trees, the pondlife, the types of birds coming to feed, and insects coming and going. I also need to stop reaching for my phone to take a photo of things and just enjoy the moments.

Finally, I have learnt that attitude is everything and it is important to be open to new ways of doing and looking at things. When I first heard about mindfulness, I was cynical and I still need a bit of convincing around meditation, but I know now that these things will never help me if my attitude does not even allow for the possibility. It is actually quite exciting to be trying and learning about new things; you never know where they might lead you.

In this chapter you have heard from...

Name: Helen Reuben
Name of company: Purple Tree Training and Coaching
Position in company / Job title: Owner
Company website: www.purpletree4u.com
Company social media handles:
Facebook: @PurpleTree4u
Twitter: @PurpleTree4u

Name: Major Pat Burgess MBE
Name of company: Ministry of Defence
Position in company / Job title: Officer Commanding Combat CIS School, AFVSR, ARMCEN Bovington, British Army
Company website: Oneworldmindfulness.co.uk
Facebook: @Oneworldmindfulness
Twitter: @PatburgessMBE

Name: John Stephenson
Name of company: Forces Transition Group
Position in company / Job title: Business Development Director
Company website: www.forcestransitiongroup.co.uk

Name: Robyn Harris
Name of Company: Equenergy: W·I·L·D Wellbeing
Position in company / Job title: Director and Soul Alignment Mentor
Company website: https://equenergy.com
Facebook page: @Equenergy and private group: https://equenergy.com/group
LinkedIn: robyn-harris-19730843 or equenergy.com/LinkedIn
Instagram: @equenergy

CHAPTER THIRTEEN

Existential Wellbeing

How often do we need to find hope or a way forward when life as we know it changes, uncertainty hits, or dreams are shattered? We cannot escape the experience of transition, loss, or uncertainty, and we cannot escape the feelings of worry, confusion, anger, fear, or grief which can occur through transitions or when we lose something important to us. This is where Grow-Beyond Founder Belinda van Zyl can help.

"Grow-Beyond provides individual as well as organisational coaching for those who wish to improve their wellbeing during periods of change or grief. The aim is to work in partnership, so life and workplace challenges are negotiated with success. This can be broken down into three key services. The first is Grow-Beyond Transitional Coaching which is individual or organisational coaching enabling clients to renew their perspectives, restore hope and find new ways of being so wellbeing is improved.

The second is Grow-Beyond Leadership Resilience Coaching which is mental-toughness coaching to move leaders from transition phases to claim greater success. The third is my Mentoring Service which enables organisations such as health care providers, educational institutions, and local authorities to consider how best to support individuals navigating transition, loss, or uncertainty. Tools, tips, and strategies are provided to support those in frontline care, line management positions, or those in Human Resources," says Belinda.

While it can be difficult, personal loss can lead us to find new purpose as we make sense of the disorientating experience, transition or loss. "This happened to me and my journey has led me to specialise as a transformational coach," she says. "I grew up in apartheid South Africa where power was given to the selected few. Whilst studying for a career in Marketing and Business Management, I was caught up in several violent attacks and protests, which contributed to a temporary loss of health."

This series of 'disorientating dilemmas' gave Belinda a fresh perspective on life, and while it ended her career in marketing, it led her to follow her heart in wanting to support people. Belinda changed her career path, firstly becoming a social worker, and later a mentor and coach. As a social worker she was involved in re-addressing power imbalances, working with the marginalised groups and initiating outcomes to enable the disempowered to gain a voice.

"As a UK social worker, I seized the opportunity to work with families who had children with disabilities. A large proportion of my early social work career was leading local initiatives to enhance social inclusion for those who were marginalised. In 2010, I became a volunteer for a large national bereavement charity enabling me to develop my interest around loss, grief and transition. To date, I remain a volunteer with this charity working with adult and child bereavement and those experiencing the impact of suicide," says Belinda.

"Currently, I work as a university lecturer as well as manage my private coaching and mentoring practise. It is hard to imagine that we can ever achieve wellbeing following a loss of someone or something important to us, but we can, with time and the right support. Throughout our life we change and adapt with every experience leaving a mark. This adaptation is sometimes referred to as building resilience, but resilience does not always equate to a sense of wellbeing."

Belinda's coaching focuses on creating that greater sense of wellbeing following change or grief. "Grow-Beyond coaching sessions acknowledge that following a loss or transition, the person we desire to be, might differ from the picture or image we originally had of ourselves before. This is because our original self-image can become distorted or lost. This can also happen when we are moving into leadership positions where we may need to become someone different. This transition can impact our wellbeing as we try to establish who we are as a leader," she says.

Grow-Beyond coaching sessions enable clients to renew or re-establish who they wish to be going forward. The approach allows clients to grow consciously through increased self-awareness. Part of this growth addresses a client's sense of being, how they want to be, and who they choose to be, following change or grief. The client is then supported to step into the embodied sense of self. Finding one's sense of self, following a transition or loss, can lead to greater self-compassion, with research evidencing that greater self-compassion promotes wellbeing.

"It is important to remember that loss is a natural part of our lifecycle, and at times, loss can place us in a spin, disorientating us and causing unimaginable grief. Recognising that these feelings are perfectly normal is the first step to improved wellbeing," says Belinda. "Feelings of fear, uncertainty, disorientation, pain, anger and even numbness are also perfectly normal. At times, these feelings might feel like a tidal wave which cannot be stopped. To be honest, they should not be stopped. Grief is a natural part of loss and it is ok to allow yourself time to grieve. Some may grieve for short periods, and others several years or even a lifetime."

What can be done to improve wellbeing when someone is lost in the no-man's land of a transition or loss? Loss encompasses so many aspects of the self. There is physical aspect, but loss also impacts us on social, psychological, and emotional levels. Belinda has put together a few ideas to help improve wellbeing after grief. The first is naming the physical elements whilst also recognising the psychological. By naming and placing words around the loss we can grieve that it more easily because we can begin to see how complex the matter is. We are not just grieving the physical, we are grieving on a much deeper emotional level.

"As part of the healing process there is value in not only acknowledging the physical loss, the 'what' have I lost, but also the psychological part, the 'what ideal' have I lost. For instance, a spouse who loses their partner through separation, divorce, or death physically loses that individual but psychologically they lose the thought of growing older with a companion. They lose shared plans and dreams; they lose their role or even sense of belonging. A new identity may need to be crafted to fit into social or cultural norms of being single again, and the pain of the change becomes compounded," says Belinda.

"The second piece of advice is to confront the loss. To grieve means to engage in the pain of emotional of the situation, yet because emotional pain is so intense, we naturally want to protect ourselves by avoiding it. The difficulty with avoidance is that, at some point in life, the pain which has not been dealt with, will present itself. Usually, unresolved grief appears as the so-called unfinished business when we go through another obstacle in life. Here the loss screams for attention as our thoughts are invaded. When we have unresolved pain often our behaviours change, then our health and wellbeing are affected."

The solution appears to be one of confrontation where we grieve the physical but also the psychological and emotional loss. This is not to say that the pain vanishes, but grief allows us to acknowledge the pain loss brings. Belinda also advises people to grieve their lost aspirations and to know that it is ok to cry and get angry; it is all part of the grieving process. You do not need to mask suffering. While we grieve the physical, we also grieve the lost aspirations and dreams. Over time we learn to adjust, we can start to build new dreams, new aspirations, and find new hope.

"My work as a social worker has led me to observe suffering and adaptation to loss," says Belinda. "Working with parents who receive a diagnosis of a disability for their child, or the news that their child has a life limiting illness can be one of the most painful sights to observe. One watches as grief becomes a daily life experience as adjustments are made. Alongside this grief, loss is compounded as future aspirations that a parent had for that child are also lost. What I have observed is how resilient we are as humans and how living in the moment can bring small moments of lightness. By embracing these moments, joy can return."

The next piece of advice from Belinda is to put perspective around your loss. "We often hold on to memories of what was, yet these memories can become distorted when emotion is high. Sometimes we grieve the memories which may lead us to experience feelings of deep hurt, resentment or anger. These feelings are normal because our life or circumstances are different, but when we do not find ways of letting go of these intense feelings, we prevent ourselves from making new memories.

Do not give up the old memories, give up the feelings which may surround these memories, if these feelings cause harm," she says.

"Then find new aspirations. Do not let broken dreams or aspirations impact the new. There are always new possibilities on the horizon waiting to be found. My son wanted to be an osteopath and began his master's in London. However, he became unwell, and this led him to suspending his studies. It was heart-breaking watching him give up on his hoped-for career path, however, I had the advantage of experiencing a similar health loss at the same age. This meant I knew by reframing this experience, new possibilities would emerge."

It took Belinda's son a year to recover physically, and he continued to commit to reframing the negative thinking that could creep in and remind him what he had lost. Today, he is thriving with a greater level of compassion and a steely determination to complete a degree in psychology. His year-long recuperation allowed him to enter the world of positive psychology and wellbeing, and he now applies what he has learnt to support struggling university students as a mentor. Whilst this was a difficult journey of loss, he found new possibilities and new aspirations which has led him to a more fulfilling career path.

Belinda's final piece of advice is to build your support system, so you are not alone. "Knowing you are not alone is a good step to greater wellbeing. Even though we may believe that we are alone on the painful journey of loss, there are people who can help and who have also shared a similar loss. Use your established network to help you manage the difficult times or find a community who cares and understands the pain of loss. There are numerous support groups and with technology improving, communities to do not have to be restricted to your area. There are even international communities who offer support, guidance, and a listening ear, you just need to find them and connect," she says.

One such coach is Suzanne Barbour of Barbour Coaching. Suzanne works with people who are or have experienced life changing illness or injury and may be struggling to cope with their diagnosis or with changes in their relationship, or with simply moving forward. Suzanne also has a free e-book on her website which offers a lot of tips on how to stay in the driver's seat during testing times.

"As someone who has experienced profound grief, as well as being a veteran, a divorcee, and a cancer survivor, I decided to pull those experiences, plus my 20-plus years in management, coaching, and mentoring, and become a Life Coach. I realised when I was going through my own cancer diagnosis that, while there was amazing support for the physical elements of my illness, the mental and practical support was sorely lacking," she says. "I decided that I wanted to be that person for other people who were going through similar situations; to plug that gap in support, and help people stay motivated to heal and move forward in whatever way that looks for them."

Suzanne believes that wellbeing needs a holistic approach, and so not only encourages good mental health practises and skills to develop resilience, but also looks at the physical aspects of person's health; from how they eat, their sleep patterns, interests, and activity level. "All of these things play an important part in person's overall mental wellbeing but often go unaddressed. I very much tailor solutions to each client based on their situation," says Suzanne.

"If I were to offer any advice, it would be first, have the conversation with your family or the people that need to know. Talking about your diagnosis can make a huge difference as trying to hide it or not worry your loved ones will only cause you more anxiety, which can be detrimental to recovery. Then, make sure you are surrounding yourself with the right people that can help you and keep you supported. Of course, I would recommend that a coach be one of those people."

Finally, Suzanne advises people to do what is best for them. "When you are putting things in place to help yourself, do what works for you. Listen to your body and, of course, your trusted advisors such as your medical team. Everyone is different with different values, so whatever you do to help yourself, make sure you set yourself up for success by weighing your options and choosing the one that works best for you."

Fay Petcher runs Feel Positive Coaching, which is a small business offering divorce, infidelity and relationship coaching, and life and holistic coaching. "I offer holistic and humanistic coaching, and counselling to both individuals and couples via Online platforms, face-to-face, and walk and talk therapy. I also offer programs to suit individual clients which include: The Healing programme, The Rebuilding Trust programme, The

Moving On programme, The Find your Passion programme, and The Reconnection programme," she says.

"Over the past 17 years, I have navigated two divorces and healed from infidelity, abuse and trauma, and PTSD, to get to a place of happiness, acceptance, peace, and fulfilment. My journey was not a linear one and neither was it a short one, but I got there. I wanted to help and empower other people who are on their own healing journey, whether that is because of relationship trauma such as abuse, toxic cycles, abandonment, or self-sabotage; or healing after infidelity or heartbreak due to relationship breakdown. I believe that everyone has the right to happiness and fulfilment."

Fay believes that developing and maintaining good mental health and wellbeing is paramount to healing and making positive steps forward after relationship breakdown, divorce, or trauma. "It is at the core of what I do when coaching clients. I promote wellbeing on all of my social media accounts through positive affirmations, quotes, tips, my own experiences, and education around things like trauma bonds and co-dependency in relationships. I offer talks to local women's groups and co-host a weekly divorce club on 'Clubhouse', where we talk about acceptance, forgiveness and moving on from a mental health and wellbeing perspective," she says.

Her book How to Succeed after Separation and Divorce has a chapter on mental health and wellbeing, and it is a theme that runs through the book as a whole, and Fay has offered us some further tips and advice for increasing hope after relationship breakdown. "First and foremost, I would advise everyone to have self-compassion and love for themselves. Secondly, to forgive yourself for the choices you have made in your relationship which had a negative impact on you and the people around you. Thirdly, to have a support network of family and friends that you can 'lean' on when you need to, whether that be help with the shopping or just a friendly ear to listen."

Next, Fay suggests practising gratitude and affirmations to develop self-worth and love. This can include saying to yourself things like: "I am worthy", "I am strong" or "I deserve love" and they are good starting points. "Also, get out in nature as much as possible, whether that is for exercise, a nature bath, outdoor meditation, or just because. Nature has a positive impact on mental health and wellbeing. Try walking barefoot in your garden to reconnect with the ground beneath your feet," says Fay.

"My next piece of advice is to practise breathing exercises and yoga which have a beneficial effect on mental health conditions and healing trauma. Breath work and yoga help us to connect to both our breathing and our bodies which are things that trauma can throw off-balance. People suffering from low mental health can feel 'disconnected' from themselves. Try to make time for the things and people that make you happy; dance in the kitchen if that is your thing, or have a regular meet up with friends. And do things that make you laugh as much as you can. Laughing at yourself when things go wrong is a way of building your resilience and learning from your mistakes."

Finally, Fay believes in the power of writing down thoughts or feelings. Journaling will free up overwhelming emotions, thoughts and feelings that are taking up space in your head. Jotting down words, thoughts or feelings will allow you to concentrate on the here and now whether that is having a cup of tea or just sitting in the garden. If you can, have a coach or counsellor to work through any blocks that are stopping you from moving forward, to gain awareness of yourself as a unique individual, to get a different perspective on your situation, and to allow you to come to your own solutions and have autonomy over your life.

One non-profit business offering holistic treatments and interventions for a range of needs is Breathe Therapies. "We provide a needs-based personal assessment and, following this, a person-centred bespoke package of care and other services. Our team are highly qualified, experienced, and professional; furthermore, they genuinely care about your experience and your wellbeing. Breathe Therapies offer six pathways: eating disorders, mental health, obesity, wellbeing, corporate mental health and wellbeing, and virtual therapy," says Clinical Director Shelley Perry.

"Many years ago, I had an eating disorder as a result of alcohol abuse, and emotional and physical abuse in my home growing up, along with sexual abuse as a child, and much family dysfunction and breakdown. With support from my church, my GP, cognitive behavioural therapy, person-centred counselling, and friends I was able to completely recover. I was unwell for four years and in therapy for two years before I recovered. I suffered from severe depression, anxiety, low self-esteem, and attempted suicide. I was determined to recover so that I could be a mental health nurse and help others in a professional capacity."

Shelley qualified as a mental health nurse in 1996 and has since specialised in eating disorders and obesity, as well as mental illness. "I am passionate about wellbeing and complete recovery. I am a widow and have been since my daughter was three years-old and my husband drowned. I then became unwell with myalgic encephalomyelitis (ME) also known as chronic fatigue syndrome (CFS), fibromyalgia on the back of a late diagnosis of Coeliac Disease, along with psychological and physical trauma from a car accident which required intensive physiotherapy for six months. It took another ten years to get the diagnosis of Coeliac Disease, M.E and fibromyalgia whilst struggling as a single mum," she says.

"I was on my own journey of research to understand what was going on with my health and what would help. I was able to recover completely from M.E and fibromyalgia and manage the Coeliac Disease so that I am healthy and well. I am completely pain free and able to run a charity and treatment clinic to help others. My passion for complete recovery for my clients is real. My advice to someone looking to improve their wellbeing is to write down your needs in terms of biology, emotions and mental health, and relationships, and seek out the most qualified and experienced practitioners."

Shelley and the team at Breathe Therapies believe that your health and wellbeing is the most precious and valuable asset you have, and is worth your time and money. Therefore, Shelley advises against going with the cheapest or the first support you come across, but to do your research. "We help develop wellbeing by firstly seeking to understand the holistic bio-psycho-social needs of the individual. For this reason, we offer an in-depth assessment to really get to know our clients. From there, our specialist, qualified, and experienced practitioners will address each need with a solution. Get it right and you will be the best version of you, living your best life," she says.

The challenges of grief, loss, ill health, relationship breakdown, and poor mental health are not only reserved for adults, nor are their consequences. The JEP Youth Engagement offers young people between the ages of eight and eighteen a unique opportunity to take an active role in shaping their futures. Founder and Director of Youth Engagement Jamie Pilling knows all too well, from his personal life experiences (an ex-offender and PE teacher) and having worked with young offenders, the impact on hope and existential wellbeing from the way young people are treated.

"By treating every young person with the respect they deserve, rather than just another 'troubled individual' to be managed through the system, we help them to develop the skills, attitude, and resilience they need to make a positive contribution to their lives, families, and communities. We help them to address their challenges in a safe environment, which in turn, enables them to be fully equipped with everything they need to fulfil their potential in the future," says Jamie.

"JEP Youth Engagement is made up of positive role models with whom young people can relate, build rapport and aspire to emulate. Young people are at the heart of everything we do, helping us shape the services we offer and how we offer them. Unlike other organisations, we do not just plug holes and move the problem along. Instead, we build long lasting relationships whilst demonstrating and delivering real, tangible results. The long-term impact we expect to see is improved academic outcomes and life choices."

JEP Youth Engagement is dedicated to supporting vulnerable young people to change their lives. They offer mental health workshops, one-to-one bespoke mentoring, and outreach work with the most at risk and challenging teenagers Jamie believes that things like exercise and sport, eating well, doing things you enjoy, taking time to relax, writing down or talking about how you feel, positive relationships, and socialising with friends and family can all help to develop positive existential wellbeing in young people. "With the right mix of opportunity, respect, dedication, and commitment, we believe that every young person has the ability to reach their full potential," he says.

Chapter summary

I imagine when I first used the phrase 'existential wellbeing' it frightened or confused people, as we were somehow expected to understand the meaning of life in order to be well. Thankfully, that is not the case. In this chapter our contributors have taken us through a number of scenarios that without the presence of hope for the future, could potentially swallow us up in pit of despair. Injustice, critical illness, relationship breakdown, abuse, and lack of opportunity can all be soul destroying if not properly healed.

But each of the stories you read about here is also one of personal triumph, of overcoming, of seeking help or support, and in turn, becoming that help or support for others; the torch of hope passed from one survivor to another so that the journey is less lonely and more bearable. It is a great comfort to know that for every story of loss, pain, grief, and sadness in the world, there are also stories of victory, not just for the individual but for the wider community. There is very much a pay-it-forward feel to it.

I believe there is no problem that cannot be solved without the right support. The hardest part is reaching out for that support, especially if hope feels like it has abandoned you. I understand what a dark and terrifying place it is when you can see no way forward, no tomorrow, no possible way of things ever getting better. If that is how you feel right now, I can guarantee you that it will not always feel this way; the light will start to find its way in again and things will get brighter. I promise. But for now, you must do the last thing you feel like doing which is to reach out and find help. Talk to someone, anyone. I know it is hard, but it will give you the best chance of recovery.

To everyone else I want to ask how can you be the hope for others? How can you be the light in someone else's life? How can you improve your own existential wellness by improving it for someone else? I am not saying you have to start your own business or charity, although if you wanted to that is great, but you could volunteer, you could text a mate and see how they are doing. You could even do something as simple as smile at a stranger. You never know what someone else is going through so simple kindness and care can make all the difference.

I do not know about you, but even just reading a chapter about hope has given me hope. It has given me a chance to reflect on some of the tough times I have experienced and the things that have got me through. It has allowed me to pause and be grateful for those things in my life, and to ponder how I can actively demonstrate that gratitude. Most of all it has given me a renewed sense of purpose in the work that I do and the way that I support others; there is work still to be done here.

In this chapter you have heard from...

Name: Belinda van Zyl
Name of company: Grow-Beyond- Coaching, Mentoring and Training
Position in company / Job title: Founder of Grow-Beyond
Company website: www.grow-beyond.co.uk
Facebook: @growbeyondcoaching
Twitter: @GrowBeyondNow

Name: Suzanne Barbour
Name of company: Barbour Coaching
Position in company / Job title: Life Coach/Founder
Company website: www.barbourcoaching.life
Facebook: @barbourcoaching
Instagram: @suzannebarbourcoaching
LinkedIn: Suzanne Barbour Coaching

Name: Fay Petcher
Name of company: Feel Positive Coaching
Position in company / Job title: Founder / Divorce, Infidelity and Relationship
Coach
Company website: www.feelpositivecoaching.com
Facebook: @feelpositivecoaching
Instagram: @feelpositivecoaching
Twitter: @feelpositivecoaching.com @faypetcher

Name: Shelley Perry
Name of company: Breathe Therapies
Position in company / Job title: Clinical Director
Company website: www.breathetherapies.co.uk
Facebook: @breathetherapies
Instagram: @breathe_therapies
Twitter: @breathetherapy

Name: Jamie Pilling
Name of company: JEP Youth Engagement
Position in company / Job title: Founder and Director of Youth Engagement

CHAPTER FOURTEEN

Transcendental Wellbeing

Whilst imagination and inspiration can be found in the here and now, it can also be beneficial to engage with things that take you somewhere else. "Literature can play and important part in our lives," says Author Caroline James. "By reading literature, we are able to see the world through the eyes of others, which in everyday life is important because it connects the reader to new experiences. Literature defines events, it creates feelings, and transmits knowledge. Each book we read can enable us to experience another life lived."

Through reading we travel to other spheres and learn about different cultures, we feel empathy or loathing for characters and experience their joy and pain. Providing an escape from monotony and giving us pleasure, literature rewards us by expanding our mind. Fiction connects us with new individuals and places, and by reading through the pages, the reader can escape from boredom and, for a moment, lead a different life.

"My father always taught me to have a dream and to ensure that I made that dream come true. From an early age my dream was to write novel, but I never thought that I was good enough. Instead, I found that I read. In fact, I read a lot. Through reading, I gained confidence and ultimately, I wrote my first novel. More have followed and my writing dream has come true. I began writing full-time in my middle years and I know that it has helped me overcome many challenges during that time," says Caroline.

"As an author I find writing incredibly helpful in reducing stress. Writing activates neurons in your brain and can act as a warm-up before tackling the day. Reading can help with our mental health too. It is proven to lower heart rate, ease tension and can even reduce stress. Reading before bed clears the mind and readies the body for sleep. A novel can improve brain function by calming the nerves and keeping the reader mentally alert. Our memory improves when we read, and science has shown that reading helps with depression and reduces the onset of Alzheimer's in later life."

Caroline recommends keeping a journal and writing two or three pages of anything that comes into your mind as soon as you get up. "Through writing any stress is left on the page. Keeping in shape applies to your mind as well as your body, and writing activates different cognitive processes which in turn unlock your creativity. Keeping your brain active through writing can help prevent mental illnesses. If you too have a dream, perhaps through writing, I hope that your dream comes true," she says.

Another creative person whose childhood dream became a reality is Su Menzies-Runciman, Owner and Artist at Su Melville Art. "I loved art as a child, but I put my pencils down when life took over and I did not pick them up again until I had a minor breakdown after the end of my marriage in 2006. I am a qualified accountant and was at executive level in a large manufacturing company, so a demanding job coupled with two small children and significant financial pressure led my body to telling me it was time to stop for a bit. In the few weeks I had off work I was told to do something for myself to help de-stress," she says.

"My mother has always been a keen artist and had sent me some paints, so I took the time to paint myself a picture. This had a twofold benefit as I had blank walls in my new home and no money for art. I discovered that I would lose myself in the painting and found myself relaxing and basically becoming a nicer person, according to my children. I did not have net curtains and at the time lived opposite a school. Unbeknown to me they were always watching my progress. A few days after I had finished that first painting, a note popped through my door asking if I did commissions. I took a leap of faith and said yes. This started a wonderful business in art."

Su found that the commissions meant she could afford art supplies and even meals out and holidays with her kids. It became her lifeline and now it is her life. She discovered that not only did she love to paint, but also loved showing other people that they could too. Now Su has four offerings as part of her business. The first, is professional quality pastel art kits which are great to rekindle your love of art. Each kit contains everything you need including an instruction booklet and access to an online tutorial.

The second, is corporate wellbeing one hour lunch and learn art sessions which are delivered to companies as part of their wellbeing programmes. In addition, Su can offer longer workshops for away days and team building events. Thirdly, Su takes a limited number of commissions every year in addition to exhibiting across the UK. You can book a commission via the contact form on her website. You can also purchase prints of her work in the print shop which is also on the website.

Finally, Su holds monthly Zoom and in person workshops across the North West. These sessions use the art kits so everyone has the correct materials and can take the kits home to create more art after the workshop. You can also book a private workshop as a birthday activity which is great via Zoom if you have family all over the globe. "Art is about recording what you see and then playing with colours, marks and other techniques. You will be pleasantly surprised with what you can accomplish in a short amount of time," she says.

"Art is a wonderful way of getting into a flow state of mind, which according to studies is a way of defining human happiness. Art also stimulates the brain creating new neuro pathways which enables you to go back into your work environment refreshed. It can also often give you a new viewpoint on your work which can increase creative problem solving and out of the box thinking. Art as part of a varied wellbeing programme helps to create a happier workforce who in turn learn techniques they can take into all areas of life."

Such techniques also increase resilience and reduce stress. This, in turn, can reduce the time taken to recover from stress-related illness and often prevents someone getting to the stage of stress which requires time off work. "Having spent most of my career in Finance and IT, my art business has a unique aspect; I understand businesses and can see the issues stress has on business costs, along with the benefits that resilience has on individuals working in pressured environments. The programmes I offer are designed to complement the individual company's wider wellbeing programme," says Su.

"My advice when it comes to art is: do not compare yourself with old masters such as Van Gogh or Degas, etc. These guys spent years immersed in nothing but art. Comparison is one of the biggest creativity killers and as adults we subconsciously do it all the time. However, like everything, if you want to do more, the key is regular practice. Doodle five minutes every day, whether that is in meetings, on the bus, waiting to pick the kids up or anywhere you find yourself with five minutes. Always keep a small notebook and a pen or pencil with you."

Also passing on their creative skills to others is Director and Owner of Sew Confident Chorley, Dawn Elliott. "I run various sewing and craft classes from my studio space in Chorley town centre. I have classes from beginners who have never used a sewing machine to advanced dressmaking. We have overlocker classes, quilting classes, knitting, crochet, and hand embroidery classes. We also do soft furnishing classes which involves learning how to make your own curtains, blinds, and lampshades. Our seasonal classes are very popular such as the arm knitting class where you knit a giant chunky blanket in just two and a half hours," she says.

"We cater for men, women and children aged eight and over, and we offered virtual classes during the Covid-19 lockdown, some of which will continue once we re-open. We have a small haberdashery area in the studio selling fabric and haberdashery items we use in our classes. I also have an Elna and Janome account so can sell sewing machines too. It is great to try out the machines in the studio before you buy. We have a mini website selling more items online including fabric, haberdashery items and craft kits which have helped to keep people sane during these strange times."

Like Caroline and Su, Dawn loved her craft as a child, but it did not become her full-time business until later in life. "I did textiles GCSE, but then took the safe route and did business studies and accountancy at University. I went form office job to office job until ten years ago when I landed a role as an office manager for an engineering company. It was a secure, well paid job and I was doing well but decided money was not everything. A number of years ago I was discussing GCSE options with my eldest child and was telling her to do what makes her happy. It made me think, I am not happy, I want a job I love and enjoy," says Dawn.

"I had always fancied running my own business. Over the years, I had done night classes at college and while I was looking at my options, I realised there was nowhere in my local area to go and do sewing etc. After a lot of Google searches and researching ideas, I discovered Sew Confident, and they were looking for franchisees. To cut a long story short, it was the perfect thing for me, and in July 2019 I opened the first Sew Confident studio in England. I love my job; it is hard work, but it is so much fun and so rewarding."

Sewing and being creative is so therapeutic and great for your wellbeing. People lead such busy, stressful lives these days, and you need to have somewhere you can go to switch off and have some well-deserved downtime. "Our hand embroidery classes are extremely popular and great for your wellbeing. You can pick up one of our embroidery kits and sew on a plane, train, at home, in the garden, anywhere really. Having something to do that uses your hands is great for dexterity and for your mind. It also gets you away from technology and snacking too," says Dawn.

"Many of my customers have found a new love of sewing after coming to the beginners sewing classes in Chorley. Some have even started their own small creative business. Coming to a class gives them the opportunity to learn a new hobby, find something for their 'me time' and get that sense of achievement from finishing a project, which is amazing. Our classes are mindful, and we have a very social environment at our studio. We encourage chatting and we have plenty of brews and biscuits during our classes, and it does not end after the class. We have great community 'Sewcial' groups on Facebook for support and chat afterwards too."

These types of activities also link with Social Wellbeing as they are great for making friends when people move into a new area, or when kids grow up and start doing their own thing and you need something to focus on. There is also a link to Environmental Wellbeing as Dawn is finding that more people are concerned about being more eco-friendly and more sustainable, so they want to start learning a new skill like upcycling to make things for themselves and their homes.

"I think anyone can learn to sew and should give it a try; sometimes you just need that little bit of confidence and some reassurance. Some people like yoga and meditation, but did you know sewing can put you in a meditative state? You need to find something you enjoy and allow yourself 'me time' or 'down time' to improve your wellbeing. I teach many of the classes in Chorley and encourage people to get involved, and say how great it is for your wellbeing. I still have stressful days and I find going to my sewing machine and making something, or picking up my hand embroidery or knitting really switches my brain off and really makes me feel better," says Dawn.

"I have sometimes joined in on classes run by my other freelance tutors, this means I too can advance my skills by learning quilting, crocheting, and dressmaking, and I absolutely love it. I get to put myself in my customer's shoes which is one of the perks of the job. The Covid-19 pandemic has given people time to reflect on life and I think we are more aware than ever of people's struggles with mental health, so it is vital you give something a go, whether it is yoga, a new gym class, painting, or sewing. At Sew Confident we really look forward to expanding and welcoming new customers to our fun and friendly classes."

Another creative pastime, usually deemed as a solitary rather than social activity, is photography, however, Director of Cherished Memories Photography Amy Newton says otherwise. "My business improves my own sense of wellbeing in many ways, particularly by allowing me to connect with a wide range of people. Reaching out to others in the community really helps provide a purpose to my work and increases creativity, which I think is the key to maintaining focus and a happy lifestyle," she says.

Amy specialises in documentary wedding photography, family and pet portraits, new-born photography, and special occasions. She aims to capture those truly special memories that can be cherished, shared, and last a lifetime. For each of her photography services, Amy offers a range of set and bespoke packages to meet the needs of each individual. Public interaction, capturing happiness, and those truly precious moments are what makes it all worthwhile for Amy.

"My love for photography began at a very early age when I was given a polaroid camera as a present. I later went on to study photography at college and university, and as my passion grew, I knew photography was a career I had to pursue. I undertook various roles in fashion and property photography after university, but when I was offered the opportunity to photograph a wedding, it made me realise how much I love this style of photography. I realised that I could handle the pressure, which I had previously seen as daunting," says Amy.

"Portraits and new-born photography soon followed, and I have now found what I was always meant to do. Not only do I love photography, but I feel I am good at it which has increased my confidence massively. This has been proven time and time again from the five-star ratings and consistent positive feedback I receive from my clients. This increase in confidence has helped me with my own mental health, and communicating with the public on a regular basis keeps me confident and smiling. On top of this, making my clients happy certainly gives me a sense of comfort and is extremely rewarding."

Amy sees photography as a great way to help those who love the outdoors but struggle to even get out of bed in the morning. Photography is a fabulous activity that you can enjoy whilst out on a walk; the scenery and fresh air can really do wonders for those who feel negative and lack that sense of purpose. "The outdoors and the tasks that I set myself when photographing nature at times can help to clear my mind. Photography is one thing that really takes my mind off my anxiety and tendency to overthink. It seems to go away when I have something to concentrate on, and really getting engrossed in a photography shoot is ideal for this," she says.

"Photography for my clients has provided them with a chance for reflection; to think about what they find precious and capture those values. My photographs have enabled my clients to look back on their special memories and re-live those moments over and over, particularly helping during hard times such as the lockdowns of 2020. This has allowed my clients to celebrate the successes and happy times rather than concentrate on the negatives. You could use photography as a way to bring your family members or friends together; give yourself a challenge or work together to create amazing imagery. It is a great idea for the kids also."

Amy has several tips for people looking to increase the inspiration and transcendental wellbeing through photography. Her first tip is to find new ways to collaborate with others, as networking can certainly help fight any negative feelings and push you out of your comfort zone. You might not agree at first, but connecting with others can be a positive thing and it can boost your confidence. "Do not shut yourself off from the world around you, working with others helps to share that enjoyment and fun. It will also enable you to concentrate on something creative that will overpower that negative self-talk you find hard to shift. Big worries will soon become non-existent," says Amy.

"I always find ways to keep the community together by offering my support, and the response I receive shows that people are generally kind and want to help each other. I sometimes set mini photo projects that people can do with family and friends. Helping people to get together and share that enjoyment, passion, and interest might be something small, but it has a big impact on everyone involved. Also, take time to reflect on your goals and achievements. It is OK to celebrate the little things, and looking back on how much you have achieved can really give you a bit of perspective."

Amy understands that even though editing and photo shoots can get quite time consuming, it is important to allow time for yourself and not be spending hours and hours doing work. Finding a balance and organising your time effectively is great for overall wellbeing. She also advises not to be afraid of trying something new. If it does not work out, then you can move in a different direction. In order to find your passion in the photography world you need to explore and experiment, so have a go at various styles and it will become clearer over time.

Finally, Amy suggests finding something you love in the subject. "Continue to find time to explore and develop ideas as this leads to great achievements. Take a camera with you wherever you travel and capture your journeys. Create a plan of where you want to visit and what you will photograph. This will give you focus and then you can look back on the imagery which will really help lift your mood during those darker or more dull days," she says.

Our final contribution comes from PINS lead singer Faith Vern whose love of music took off when she received a guitar for Christmas when she was 12. "I had guitar lessons in the evening, once a week, and always wanted to form a band, but didn't really know anybody to form a band with, or how to do it. So, when I finished school and went to college, I then moved to Manchester, and there was a lot more opportunity to meet musicians. Initially, I was trying to join other people's bands, meeting up with them if they were doing a project and looking for a guitar player to join them. But nothing really fit," she says.

"I noticed that there was a lack of all females bands in Manchester, so I decided to put one together. I am the frontwoman of the band and have been since the beginning. I also started an independent record label with my bandmates, and I compose music for TV and film. Playing music is my passion and the drive I have for it led me to making it my job. I would make music whether I made money from it or not, so on the one hand, I would consider it a job as it pays me a wage, but on the other hand, it is still just something I feel compelled to do."

For Faith, the process of creating new material differs depending on what she is writing, but her favourite part of her work will always be playing live. "The gigging experience is probably the best bit and the reason that at least everyone in my band wants to be in a band like that. It is the whole point. When we started the band, we said to ourselves, imagine if we play at Leeds Festival, because when you are 18, it is like the rite of passage to go to Leeds festival. I never thought we would actually play it, but we did. Then, quite quickly, we were getting to play in America; New York and Los Angeles, and there were people at the shows that wanted to watch us and knew the songs," she says.

"Gigging has always been the exciting part of it. From getting in the van, packing all the stuff, and deciding your outfits, to getting into the place and having a drink with friends, or going out for a meal. It is very social because you are just with them for the entire time that you are on the tour or at the show. You also get to see the other bands that are playing, and then go out afterwards and see all the different cities, or towns, or wherever it is. The gig where we supported Stereophonics in Wrexham was particularly good because it was at a stadium, which we had never done before. It was absolutely huge crowd, and all of our families were there as well."

Faith's advice to other musicians is not to worry about receiving negative feedback in terms of record reviews and show reviews. Music is such a subjective thing that cannot, and do not, need to please everyone. Also, ignore the internet trolls as they feed on reaction. Instead enjoy what you are doing, that is why you are doing it. Remember that nerves are good as long as they do not take over, PINS always get together for a huddle and a few deep breaths before they play a show.

"I would consider listening to music and watching live music to be good for one's wellbeing. When people listen to my band's music it may make them feel a certain way. The same goes for if they come to one of our shows, they may feel uplifted or cathartic, or they may just get lost in the noise and dancing. Many young women have told me that they have started a band or picked up a guitar, or just felt braver after seeing our band, so I would like to say that I hope we promote confidence," says Faith.

Chapter Summary

As a creative individual I love that there are so many businesses out there helping to bring inspiration and imagination into the world of wellbeing. While presence and being present are fundamental to our overall health, the balance of that is the escapism and transcendence brought about by the other worlds and other places we access when we are in the creative zone. It is interesting that we understand that too much of this can be detrimental and that it can become a crutch for our avoidance strategies, yet we do not seem to put much focus on the fact that a lack of inspiration can also be unhealthy.

I think the biggest take away for me in this chapter is that you can make a living out of what you love if that is what you choose to do. Sometimes hobbies are best as just hobbies, but there is a place for creative businesses, especially if that business teaches new skills, helps build communities and social groups, or creates a sense of magic that you can revisit time and time again. So many of the other areas of wellbeing are also represented and covered in this chapter which shows how diverse and encompassing creativity can be.

The other thing I have learnt is how collaborative these things can be. All I have to do is look at this book and the number of people involved to change my perception that writing, or at least creative writing as I had experienced it so far, was a solitary endeavour. It has made me think about some of my other creative pursuits, namely crocheting the blankets that I inflict on my nieces and nephews every Christmas, and how I might be able to use that to improve my Social Wellbeing as we come out of the lockdowns of 2020 and 2021.

I think the final thing to say here is that inspiration and imagination are not restricted to the creative arts; cookery, engineering, architecture, design, and invention, all engage with these concepts too. It might be that these are the route to which you prefer to engage with Transcendental Wellbeing and that is absolutely fine. I am sure we can all find at least one way we connect with this area even if you have never thought about it that way before. The trick now is to find a way to do more of it in your life, to consciously set aside time to participate in activities that inspire you, and to recognise and acknowledge the benefits that come with it.

In this chapter you have heard from...

Name: Caroline James
Name of company: Caroline James
Position in company / Job title: Author
Company website: www.carolinejamesauthor.co.uk

Name: Su Menzies-Runciman
Name of company: Su Melville Art
Position in company / Job title: Owner / Artist
Company website: www.SuMelville.com
Facebook: @SuMelvilleArt
Instagram: @SuMelvilleArt
Twitter: @SuMelville

Name: Dawn Elliott
Name of company: Sew Confident Chorley
Position in company / Job title: Director / Owner
Company website: https://www.sewconfident.co.uk
Facebook: @SewConfidentChorley
Instagram: @sewconfidentdawn, @sewconfident
Twitter: @sewconfident

Name: Amy Newton
Name of company: Cherished Memories Photography
Position in company / Job title: Director
Company website: www.cherishedmemoriesphotography.co.uk
Facebook: @cherishedmemoriesphotography01
Instagram: @cherishedmemoriesphotography01

Name: Faith Vern
Name of company: PINS
Position in company / Job title: Lead singer
Company website: www.wearepins.co.uk or www.hausofpins.com
Facebook: @pinsmusic
Instagram: @wearepins
Twitter: @wearepins

CHAPTER FIFTEEN

Conclusion

What a privilege indeed to have so much information, advice, and guidance at our fingertips across the twelve main chapters of this book. While I have tried my best to summarise each one as we went along, my priority was always to allow as much room as possible for the contributions and save my own thoughts for the closing pages. Just as I took you though the definitions of each of the sections in Chapter 1, I will now draw one encapsulating conclusion for the 12 ways of wellbeing; hopefully, this will cement in your mind some of the things you have learnt or that have inspired you, once again, to connect with the words, advice, or individuals presented to you.

Physical Wellbeing, as with wellness in general, goes beyond just diet and exercise. It is the first section in The Wellbeing Wheel because it is the foundation for everything else, and yet so often we misunderstand it, abuse it, reject it, or neglect it, and find ways of turning it on ourselves. Reconnect with your body by getting to know yourself, your habits, your abilities, your aches and pains, your likes and dislikes, even your DNA. Then, use that information to make better, more personalised choices for yourself, your home, your family, and your health. And remember, natural, clean, and safe, is an absolute must when it comes to physical health.

Mental Wellbeing and education go hand in hand. We have come along leaps and bounds in how we view mental illness but still have a long way to go to truly eradicate the shame and stigma experienced by people who are suffering, which by the way, is a very high percentage of us in one way or another. The more I researched and understood my PTSD diagnosis the less fear I felt, and I often come across moments with clients where I can feel their relief as they realise that symptoms they are experiencing are completely normal for their condition. Learning for and about mental wellbeing, however, should be balanced with teachings on prevention and general health.

Emotional Wellbeing has two parts to it. The first, is allowing yourself to feel what you need to without judgement. This does not mean we wallow or allow our feelings to eat away at us, but to give them the space to just be. The second, is to listen to what those emotions are trying to tell you. Every emotion is a message, we just must be open enough to receive it. I know for many emotions can be an awkward or distressing thing to encounter, but as long as we can maintain a compassionate and healthy approach to them, there is nothing to be afraid of. If we reach a point where we cannot, then the ability to reach out for support is equally as important.

Relational Wellbeing is very closely linked with the notion of patterns; patterns that were created as children become patterns that play out as adults, showing themselves in our relationships time and time again. Increasing relational wellbeing involves addressing the old patterns and implementing new ones so that we can break the cycle of old wounds preventing us from experiencing full, healthy, intimate, and fulfilling relationships. But remember, these patterns are not necessarily of your making, they were also influenced by external factors and so we should first learn to treat ourselves with kindness and respect.

Social Wellbeing on a national level seems to be something we are struggling with. We only have to look at the fall-out from the European 2020 Cup final to see deep unhealed divides in society. On a more local and personal level though, the Covid-19 pandemic in general seemed to enhance feelings of community spirit and highlight the innate need we all have for connection and belonging. If increasing your social wellbeing comes from community, then the first takeaway message here should be to find your tribe; no matter who you are or what you are interested in. The second, is to then expand your reach, to befriend people that are different to you; you will gain so much from it.

Learning about Recreational Wellbeing actually really surprised me. I knew the links between recreational and social wellbeing were strong, but I did not see until that point just how far that connection went. One of the other messages that seems to have appeared a number of times around recreational wellbeing is to start with something that you used to do, something that has brought you joy before but has, for some reason, slipped from your life or routine. I used to love to sing, swim, and ride horses, even if I were to just take up one of these things again, it would have a huge impact on my recreational wellbeing as well as other areas of my life.

If I had to pick a word to go with Financial Wellbeing it would be 'advice'. If you are anything like me, things like loans, mortgages, interest rates, inflation, tax, and insurance feel very overwhelming. I have been lucky to have been able to access plenty of support around my finances particularly when it came to setting up my business, and I am very grateful for that. Improving financial wellbeing is less about getting more money and more about becoming richer with your time, and thoughts, and a sense of freedom. I suspect that for many, having enough to get by without worry or enough to provide for your family is more of a success than being wealthy.

Occupational Wellbeing is about creating physical and psychological safety for staff which can be done in so many ways. From ensuring that employees have healthy work routines and desk set ups, to offering good benefit packages, clear progression routes, embedded staff support programmes, and, most importantly, a culture of truly caring for and wanting the best for everyone. The way we work has changed and will continue to change as more and more automated systems are introduced, we need to find ways of using the talent that these systems free up rather than just the capital. Skills, knowledge, and experience need to be retained.

Environmental Wellbeing has become such a significant part of our agenda personally, nationally, and globally. Increasing our environmental wellbeing starts within, by recognising that we are a part of nature, and therefore, have a duty to act responsibly. Once we understand and accept this, our thinking changes, which therefore, impacts our decisions and behaviours. As I sit writing this, I start to see how things might be different if I made more environmentally conscious choices. While I will never turn vegetarian or vegan, I can support both the farming community and the environment by choosing locally sourced products.

Spiritual Wellbeing as a title seems so far removed from everyday life, but having explored its meaning through the lens of presence, we can see just how important and relevant it can be. Absent-mindedly driving a car or chopping up vegetables, or operating heavy machinery is a sure-fire way of having an accident. Presence not only keeps us safe, but also keeps us involved. I am, I feel, too often thinking about my next project or worrying about something when my partner and I take our dog for a walk, and if it were not for him, I would miss all wonderful moments we have of encountering nature or having great conversation. It helps to get out of your head every now and then.

Existential Wellbeing as we have said is about our hope. We have all experienced tragedy, loss, heartache, and pain in one form or another, some of which has been devastating and some we have been able to recover from quickly; either way, our belief than we can get through it, is a significant part of keeping us going. Improving existential wellbeing means digging in to and holding on to what we have, what we gained or learnt from our experiences, and knowing how we can pay it forward. There is also a large emphasis here on getting support whether that is medically and physically, or mentally and emotionally.

Finally Transcendental Wellbeing, our ability to engage with the realms of imagination and inspiration; to explore worlds beyond our own whilst sat in the comfort of our living room, or to breathe life into something new of our own creation and to share it with the people around us. It takes a tremendous amount of courage to put something out into the arena, especially when it is something new or different, or unique; it requires being very open and vulnerable to the judgement and criticism of others. However, this is how we progress. I know all too well how the creative arts are generally viewed, but all creativity and innovation are art, making it one of the most powerful tools we have.

So, what happens next? I sincerely hope that nobody finishes this book and suddenly feels like they have to start working on all 12 areas of their wellbeing at once. The point of this book was not to make anyone feel like they are lacking, or to cause panic. My advice would be to choose just one area to start with; this can be done by looking at the chapter where you learnt the most, or where the stories really stood out to you. You could also try asking yourself, if I was to improve just one area, which one would have the biggest positive impact on my wellbeing as a whole? Which one would influence the largest number of other areas in my life?

Next, I would suggest getting some help, whether that is from someone included in this book, someone you find elsewhere, or someone you already know. Having someone to support you and keep you accountable is a really great way of being able to set a healthy and realistic goal for yourself, to consistently work towards that goal, to provide you guidance, should you need it, and to celebrate the completion of that goal with you. I have said it before and I will say it again, find someone that you click with and trust, human or animal, and do not be afraid to add levels of support, or find someone new to work with if you need to.

Finally, be kind to yourself. Nobody I know has had an easy straight road to where they want to be. Stumbles happen, setbacks happen, but the only failure is giving up completely. The journey to improved wellbeing is like any other journey, taken one step at a time, and sometimes you need to rest in order to be able to carry on, and that is ok. Please do not beat yourself up when these moments come; instead, celebrate how far you have come, practice gratitude for the lessons you have learnt, and prepare for the next leg. Tell yourself that you can do this, as many times as you need to, and remember that you are not alone.

I truly hope that The 12 Ways of Wellbeing or The Four Spheres of Connection, whichever is easiest for you to remember, have been useful frameworks for you to think about wellness in a more holistic way; to understand that there is not a single area of our lives that does not impact us as a whole, and to see that even just small improvements or increases in one area can positively raise our overall levels of wellbeing. I end as I began, by saying that everything is connected, and I would love to connect with you and your stories, and to hear how this book has resonated with you in your journey. You can find all my details at the end of this chapter.

In this chapter you have heard from...

Name: Gemma Margerison

Name of Company: Gemma Margerison, Gemma Louise Coaching, and TRUCE

Position in company/Job title: Author, Inspirational Speaker, Coach, and Researcher

Company website: www.gemmalouisecoaching.com

Facebook: @gemmalouise.coaching.1

LinkedIn: https://www.linkedin.com/in/gemma-margerison-041450170/

Instagram: @gemma.margerison @gemmalouisecoaching @truce.trauma. resilience

Acknowledgements

All that is left for me to do now is to say thank you to all the people who have made this book possible.

Thank you to all of my contributors: Julia Riewald, Rebecca Woolley-Wildgoose, Adam Grayston, Kelly Farr, Robyn Ramsell, Claire Benson, Jennie Hughes, Amanda Green, Vicky Bennett, Amanda Englishby, Lisa Shannon, John Kenny, Lou Chiu, Ben Thompson, Dave Scholes, Jackie Robinson, Sean Molino, Phil Jones, Jim Prescott, Vicky Watson, Lara Bennington, Adam Kirkham, Serena Smith, Kathryn Jeacock, Justine Hodgkinson, Debbie Edwards, Maddy Lawson, Matt Gibbs, Kate Holroyd, Alex Brooke, Helen Reuben, Pat Burgess, John Stephenson, Robyn Harris, Belinda van Zyl, Suzanne Barbour, Fay Petcher, Shelley Perry, Jamie Pilling, Caroline James, Su Menzies-Runcimen, Dawn Elliott, Amy Newton, and Faith Vern.

Thank you so much for your willingness to share, your passion for what you do, and the patience you have shown as I have negotiated my way through writing and publishing a book for the very first time. Particular thanks go to those who have been a part of the Connected YouTube channel and podcast; it is much appreciated.

Additional thanks go to our sponsors Amanda Green, Cat Lawson, and Phil and Hazel Maltby. Thank you also to Mark Booker for helping to keep the book on track; to Dot Crockford for tidying it up; to Ariane

Sherine for our amazing cover design; and to Juliette Jones for getting us across the line.

Personal thanks go to Mum and Dad, Carol, and our extended families for your support; to Bee Kershaw for having been my best friend through all of the ups and downs of the last few years; and most importantly to Scott, for your unfailing love and belief in me.

Printed in Great Britain
by Amazon